FIRST
IN ASTROLOGY

The Secrets of Character
Revealed by the Stars

by

PRESTON CROWMARSH

THE AQUARIAN PRESS
Wellingborough, Northamptonshire

First published 1971
Second Edition, revised, enlarged
and reset 1984

British Library Cataloguing in Publication Data

Crowmarsh, Preston
   First steps in astrology. — 2nd ed.
   1. Astrology
   I. Title
   133.5   BF1708.1

ISBN 0-85030-391-5

*The Aquarian Press is part of the
Thorsons Publishing Group*

Printed in Great Britain by
Richard Clay (The Chaucer Press) Ltd,
Bungay, Suffolk

FIRST STEPS IN ASTROLOGY

A practical introduction to the interpretation of astrological birth charts.

CONTENTS

CHAPTER ONE

ASTROLOGY IN ACTION

This little volume is not meant to be a textbook on astrology but an aperitif to whet the appetite. Its aim is strictly limited. The idea is to introduce you to the subject painlessly and then to show, even at this elementary stage, how it is possible to know people by the movements of the planets in their charts.

Once you have mastered the rudiments your interest will quicken, and when that happens you will progress easily and rapidly. Astrology explains the reasons for events; why one is quick or slow; strong or weak; rich or poor; why one man or woman has made a huge success, and another failed.

It will explain why one woman is fat and another slim; whether a lean woman will fatten — and when. This will not be accomplished by magic, clairvoyance or intuition but by interpreting a chart with skill. A few who have a bent for the art will master it quickly; others will take much longer; some will even be baffled and relinquish the study. It depends on you. Here are a few examples of famous people, showing how the signs in their charts are interpreted.

Margaret Thatcher (13 October 1925)

She is misunderstood and under-estimated. Venus rising in Sagittarius gives her elegance and femininity; Scorpio rising at birth with Sagittarius ascending, courage and the desire for change and reform; her two professions — chemistry and the law — reflect the Scorpio influence. Saturn provides enormous stamina and resilience but also shadows her outlook with pessimism and doubt; for despite outward appearances she is not an Iron Lady, in the sense that she is inflexible. She needs reassurance, but having made up her mind is not easily turned from her purpose.

Nor is Margaret Thatcher unfeeling. Sun, Mercury and Mars forming a square with Jupiter indicates that she is open-hearted, unguarded and has much consideration for others. She feels deeply for the unemployed and suffering, but her way, she feels, is the only one that will help them.

Libra rising indicates her undoubted capacity for leadership and Sun and Mercury in conjunction endow her with exceptional mental brilliance. Her chart shows that she took high office at a critical time for the party but that she would enjoy two and a half years of unparalleled popularity, with a period to consolidate her gains.

Cyril Smith (28 June 1928)
Like so many Cancer natives he is a complex character and emotionally sensitive — making a good friend but a bad enemy. With Uranus and Jupiter conjunct he is underrated. With Aries square to Sun, Mercury and Venus he has an urge for authority and leadership but he is not a compromiser, being very much his own man, and will continue to earn the respect both of friends and enemies.

He started life in the Civil Service, took to politics, became Liberal Party agent from 1948-50; switched to Labour and was Party Agent for Ashton-under-Lyne for three years. He was prominent in local politics, became an alderman and Mayor of Rochdale in 1966. Mayors are ruled by the tenth house and Capricorn, both prominent in his chart. In 1967 he rejoined the Liberal Party and was returned for Rochdale.

Neptune in the fifth house in Leo gives him a sense

of artistic and musical appreciation and Leo on the cusp of the fifth house a love for children. He is ambitious and his Part of Fortune is so placed — Neptune in the fifth in Leo — that it should be no surprise to see him eventually in the House of Lords. Altogether, a complex, courageous and honest politician.

Prince Charles (14 November 1948)

Leo, known as the royal sign, is on the cusp of his ascendant. The Moon is in the tenth house (profession) which shows that he will be brought before the public in the course of his duties, which are multifarious. Like a typical Scorpio he is determined not to be a 'yes-man' but to take a full part in the nation's affairs within the limits permitted to royalty.

Mars in Sagittarius in the fifth house gives him a love of sport. Though not academically brilliant he is endowed with sound common sense and the desire to apply himself diligently to any study he embraces. The Sun in Scorpio on the cusp of the fifth house shows that he is interested in change and reform and novel ideas — thus his desire that the BMA should examine alternative medicine.

Sun in Scorpio gives him a flexible mind and the need to accommodate social change, and also to create change. He has a wide variety of interests. He heeds his father's advice and has shrewd judgement and a disciplined mind.

Neptune and Venus form a conjunction in Libra; as Neptune tends to enhance the feminine nature of Venus, he is sensitive to beauty and, as the world knows, has married a beauty with artistic inclinations, though with little of his love for sport.

Saturn, a symbol of tradition, is well aspected with Jupiter, the Moon and the mid-heaven vortex, so when he assumes the throne Britain will have a King who will help to guide the destiny of the Nation.

Prince Philip (10 June 1921)

Prince Philip has the royal sign of Leo on the cusp of his Ascendant, indicating powers of leadership. Had he made a career in a branch of the armed forces he would have risen to the top. Moon in his first house in conjunction with Neptune makes him intuitive, popular with the public and gives him a love of the sea. Sun in conjunction with Mars in Gemini makes him impulsive, sometimes brusque and abrasive and indicates physical and mental energy and a love for constant movement. He has travelled the world in the interests of Britain.

The Sun's conjunction with Mars in Gemini makes him irascible at times, and its square aspect with Jupiter and Saturn, which form a conjunction with Virgo, accounts for his brushes with authority and the Press. He does not speak without due reflection and consultation. He has an understanding mind and he and the Queen discuss all matters relating to the nation's affairs before she makes any important announcement. He does far more work for the nation's good (behind the scenes) than most people imagine.

Ex-President Richard Nixon (9 January 1913)

The Ex-President's Sun lies in Capricorn, the sign of the Goat — and of ambition. Like the goat, he climbed slowly and sure-footedly ever upwards. Time was of no consequence. Libra is on the cusp of his Second House (money); Venus the ruler of Libra in his Sixth House (daily work) points to his interest in law; Jupiter close to his Sun buttressed his efforts and brought him wealth. His Virgo Ascendant makes him practical; the ruler of this Ascendant is Mercury, which conjuncts Jupiter in his Sun sign. The ruler of his Sun (Saturn) is near the Mid-Heaven (Ninth House), which points to his eventual success and to his interest in the Law. Though anyone can see that Nixon would have been a success, it needs an expert to have predicted that he would reach the White House, and a very good astrologer indeed to have predicted his downfall. Yet, in retrospect, both can be seen from the signs.

Adolf Hitler (20 April 1889)

Saturn lay in his Tenth House and the cusp of the Tenth House was afflicted by the Sun and by square aspects which brought about the death of his mother. In 1933 Hitler became Chancellor of the Third Reich. Why? His chart shows that his MC is progressed by 43 so there is a wonderful aspect of Mars conjunct Venus trine progressed MC. This will be obvious when you master the rudiments of astrology and acquire a deeper knowledge of the subject.

In 1924 he was imprisoned because he had Saturn in opposition to his Sun from Scorpio. Neptune in his Eighth House (the end) accounts for his mysterious death because Neptune influences secrets, hallucinations, poisoning and self-destruction. One could write a fascinating book from Hitler's chart, tracing the various dramatic events in his life to its fitting conclusion.

The Duke of Windsor (23 June 1894)

The Duke was born with Aquarius rising and as Aquarius is progressive, enthusiastic, creative, unconventional and fond of reforms, it is easy to see why he attempted to break with tradition and create precedents. Unfortunately, British conservatism was too much for him.

The day he read his Abdication Message over the air (10 December 1936) Neptune was transitting the House of Marriage (seventh) in square with radical Jupiter, the ruler of the Tenth House (profession), which concerns, amongst other things, change of abode. Jupiter was in opposition to his Sun, and as the Sun rules the House of Marriage and Jupiter indicates position and honour, it follows that the Duke lost his position and much of the homage paid to him. It all worked out precisely as his chart showed, and was in fact, predicted by Cheiro in 1910.

Kaiser Wilhelm II (27 January 1859)

Kaiser Wilhelm II was born at 3 p.m. in Berlin. Sepharial worked out his horoscope, which he published in 1903,* a courageous act, for Wilhelm was then at the zenith of his power. He wrote:

> We find Saturn in the sign of its declivity opposing the Sun in its weakest sign; Mars and Neptune conjoined in the meridian, and the Sun semi-square to both; the malefics — Neptune, Mars and Uranus — elevated and the Moon in opposition to Uranus . . . during his reign the German Empire will suffer reversals of which hitherto it has had no shadow of experience. Kaiser Wilhelm . . . will lose nearly the whole of his possessions. He will never be a popular monarch. Mars on the meridian will cause him to engage in continual quarrels, and the Sun in opposition to Saturn will denude him of his power among nations. He will lose his royal spouse (Moon in opposition to Uranus retrograde) suddenly. Nothing more adverse or less royal than this horoscope of the Kaiser, except, perhaps, that of the Sultan of Turkey (Abdul the Damned), is to be found among the rulers of Europe. The Kaiser will die suddenly, and the heart will be the seat of the final affliction.

It needed unusual skill to work out the Kaiser's horoscope so accurately, and courage to publish his findings at a time when there was no sign whatever that the German Empire would crumble. Everything, in fact, pointed the opposite way.

---

* *Manual of Astrology:* Sepharial — Nichols & Co. 1903.

David Frost (7 April 1939)

Jupiter in Mid-Heaven is in its own sign, Pisces, trining his Moon in the Fifth House (entertainment), showing that he will be successful in the field of entertainment, as has proved to be the case. Venus on the cusp of the Tenth House, also exalted in Pisces, points to success overseas.

Mars in the Sixth House squares Mercury in the Tenth House, giving warning that he should control his tongue lest he find himself involved in libel proceedings. He also has Neptune, co-ruler of Pisces, on the cusp of the Fourth House, which rules the Ninth House (overseas), an indication that in all probability he will eventually make his home overseas. He is very ambitious and with Mercury in bad aspect to Mars there is danger that he may over-tax himself, with a resulting loss of energy and frayed nerves.

Jacqueline Kennedy/Onassis (28 August 1929)

The last degree of Scorpio on the Ascendant (Mars is the ruler of Scorpio) makes her strong willed and ambitious. Two planets, Venus and Mars in the Seventh House, point to two marriages, both to wealthy husbands. A retrograding Saturn in opposition to Venus indicates the death of her first husband.

Venus in opposition to Saturn means that there is sorrow in connection with love and another Saturn aspect to Venus shows that her second husband will be considerably older. Saturn in the First House gives her a considerable degree of self-control, which she exercised when her first husband, John F. Kennedy, died.

Charlie Chaplin (16 April 1889)

At first glance one would hesitate to say that Chaplin would be not only very wealthy but world famous, as he laboured under severe handicaps. His chart shows

Moon square Saturn; Moon opposition Mars; Mars square Saturn; Mercury opposition Uranus; and Sun opposition Uranus. Consult the chapter on aspects and you will see how frustrating and inhibiting these are. His life was a triumph of personality and character, and Sun and Mercury in Aries gave him courage, initiative and an adventurous nature.

Four planets in his Seventh House indicate his four marriages, the first three ending in divorce, with the fourth successful because Venus was in Taurus, its own sign.

His success is shown by Jupiter in the Second House (money) in Capricorn. The ruler of Capricorn (Saturn) is near the Mid-Heaven in Leo, the sign of entertainment; Sun, ruler of Leo, is in his Sixth House (work), a pointer to his profession — a supreme entertainer.

Moon on the cusp of his Ascendant brings his personality dramatically to the fore, for not only did he act in films, but wrote the scripts, composed the music — and sang!

Astrology in Real Life

Happiness and contentment is the aim in life for everyone and to find out how to achieve this, many people visit astrologers. Unfortunately, most men confuse happiness with money, position and power; women identify it with a good marriage, but these will not necessarily bring contentment.

A big bank balance does not necessarily lead to happiness; nor marriage to a partner to whom one is unsuited. Work is the most precious thing in the world and an astrologer can advise you about the work for which you are best fitted.

One Christmas Eve I had a letter from a man who said he was earning a very fat salary 'in a job which I loathe', and asked whether he should throw it up and become a writer on the strength of some thirty or forty articles he had sold to trade and other magazines.

The letter filled me with gloom because when I was young I trained to be an engineer but escaped in my twenties to carve out a career in writing. But at fifty-three! I doubted whether he could have endured hardship and penury at that age, especially after being accustomed to a handsome wage. I examined his chart but could see no success as a writer, so reluctantly wrote and told him so.

Consult An Astrologer About Your Children

Parents who have their children's interests at heart — and who hasn't? — should consult a *reputable* astrologer, who will say what they are fitted for. I know a man who loved music. His parents sent him to Harrow and Clare College, Cambridge, and when after dabbling in the humanities and totally unfitted for business, they looked round for a job for him. His father, a baronet and a retired Indian Army general, found a niche for him in an engineering firm of which he was a director.

One morning the manager spotted the young man doing a routine job. 'Why are you wearing that tie?' he asked.

'Why not? I was at Clare.'

The manager had been at Clare, too, and the Old School Act was put into operation. The young man found himself in a responsible position in the Production Department, where he made such a hash of things that he was soon out on his ear. His next job was in a garage.

Eventually after many failures he found a job with a firm of music publishers and rapidly rose to the top. Had his parents consulted an astrologer he could have been groomed for a music career and been saved many years of frustration and hardship.

Research Into Astrology

Every parent should read *Astrology — Thirty Years Of Research* by Doris Chase Doane, which gives details of thousands of horoscopes which she has analysed. Her results prove conclusively that the signs and aspects indicate clearly the inclinations the natives* have, the professions they are fitted for, the diseases to which they are prone, the types of people to whom marriage would result in happiness, and a host of other valuable details.

The value of astrology lies in guiding a child into the right profession; in choosing the right partner; and in helping people to avoid disease. When the young are in love they are in a state of temporary insanity and unlikely to heed the advice of parents, or an astrologer. In middle age and after, marriage often takes place for a variety of reasons which have nothing to do with love. In the case of women it is often for security; with men financial interests usually predominate. Astrological advice is seldom heeded until it is too late. Where children are concerned, however, helping to choose the right profession is of paramount importance.

CHAPTER TWO

THE SIGNS

Though originally all astrologers studied astronomy, which is the mother science, it is not necessary for the student of astrology to know any but the most elementary facts about astronomy.

In order to erect a horoscope you should know that the Zodiac is a belt of the celestial sphere 8 or 9 degrees

* The native is the person whose chart has been drawn up and whose horoscope has been read.

on each side of the ecliptic, within which the apparent motions of the Sun, Moon and principal planets (not stars) take place; that it is divided into twelve equal parts called Signs which are named after twelve constellations; and that the Signs of the Zodiac do not change their places. Below are given the traditional names of the Signs, their English equivalents, symbols and characteristics.

Name	E.E.	Symbol	Characteristic
Aries	Ram	♈	Fire
Taurus	Bull	♉	Earth
Gemini	Twins	♊	Air
Cancer	Crab	♋	Water
Leo	Lion	♌	Fire
Virgo	Virgin	♍	Earth
Libra	Balance	♎	Air
Scorpio	Scorpion	♏	Water
Sagittarius	Archer	♐	Fire
Capricorn	Goat	♑	Earth
Aquarius	Waterman	♒	Air
Pisces	Fishes	♓	Water

From this it will be seen that there are three fire, earth, air and water signs, which simply means that those born under these signs are endowed with characteristics generally associated with them. But of course, character reading is not as simple as all that and many other factors have to be weighed and considered.

The signs bestow characteristics, qualities and talents, good and bad, on those born under them. Fortunately no human is either wholly good not utterly bad and numerous interacting influences decide what a person will be. These we shall discuss later but in this chapter we will deal with the influences of the Signs. Aries is always considered first as the 21 March is the start of the astrological year.

Aries the Ram ♈ 21 March-20 April: *Fire Sign*.

The Good Aries: The Sign shows the horns of the ram, and like this animal he will be determined, impulsive, charged with ambition, fire and courage, ready to go bald-headed for anyone or anything; energetic and independent. Under Aries one finds travellers, sportsmen, leaders, explorers, people ever ready to fight and act. To them the blackest clouds are edged with gold for they are the world's optimists. They are clever, think quickly and in debate their retorts come back with the speed of snapping elastic. Nature has given them a sense of dry humour, which makes them excellent company, and they are thorough in all undertakings.

Bad Aries: Here determination turns to pig-headedness, impulsiveness to rashness and energy, instead of being diverted into creative channels, degenerates into restlessness. The native is too quick, acting first; regretting later. Here ambition is corrupted into greed and a desire for power; energy takes the form of aggression; irony turns into sarcasm. Because he acts much too hastily he has ample time for regret; because he rides roughshod over others who think more slowly, he earns a reputation for rudeness, brusqueness, lack of consideration and even vindictiveness. He rarely completes any undertaking.

Well-Known Aries Natives
Bette Davis, Harry Houdini, Robert the Bruce, Vandyck, Laplace, William Harvey, Thomes Hobbes, Rousseau, J. S. Mill, Grotius, Hazlitt, Van Gogh, Joan Crawford, Cobden, Sir Adrian Boult, Mary Pickford, William Morris, J. S. Bach, Hans Andersen, Karl Marx, A. C. Swinburne, Duke of Wellington, Balzac, Tchaikovsky.

The reader might say that astrology does not make sense if people of such diverse types and varying abilities all come under the same sign. This, however, is the only Sun sign which, while having a significant influence on the native often has its power modified by the Ascendant and other powerful aspects. This you will realize as you progress and master succeeding stages of the subject.

Taurus the Bull ♉ 21 April-20 May: *Earth Sign*.

Good Taurus: The sign depicts a bull's head and horns because the native is simple, natural, transparently honest and exudes kindness. He is a sound plodder who reaches his goal by sheer concentrated effort, no matter how long it may take. Such people love harmony, colour, pleasant surroundings, and revel in good food. They usually have melodious singing and speaking voices and can be exceedingly charming. Many gravitate to the arts, especially singing, music and painting. Taurus wives make attractive homes and both sexes are faithful, loyal and uncomplicated.

Bad Taurus: Lack of reason and stubbornness associated with the bull are characteristics of this primitive type. You can't argue with them for once they've made up their minds nothing will shift them. Love of food turns them into gluttons. They are avaricious; money and possessions come first; can't be trusted and are reactionary in outlook, politically and socially. Because they are stupid and will not be advised many become fanatics. Unlike the good Taurus who gets there by effort this type is lazy, slovenly, and jealous of those who succeed.

Well-Known Taurus Natives
Queen Elizabeth II, Shakespeare, Henry Fielding, Kant, Gibbon, Fahrenheit, Edward Jenner, Karl Marx, Yehudi Menuhin, Cecil Day Lewis, Queen Juliana, Joseph Whitaker, Harry S. Truman, H. E. Bates,

Barbra Streisand, Thomes Hobbes, Trollope, Sir Arthur Sullivan, Hitler, Machiavelli, William Booth, Baudelaire.

Gemini the Twins ♓ 21 May-21 June: *Air Sign*.

Good Gemini: The quickest thinkers of all; versatile, vivacious, intelligent, adaptable. Their minds are like quicksilver, darting, changing course, spotting the solutions of problems in a flash. No matter what turns up they can handle it. Avoid getting into a slanging match with one unless you're absolutely sure of your ground, or he will turn you inside out. But they are witty and reasonable, make fine linguists, work hard because it is their nature to do so, and revel in words and books. Because of this they make excellent journalists, especially gossip writers, for they are good critics and excel in ferreting out secrets. They are at home in any profession that has to do with writing and expression and are exceedingly versatile. They make good secretaries and solicitors, too.

Bad Gemini: Here quick thinking results in superficiality. They cannot stay at any job long enough to make a success of it. Studies are left unfinished, solutions unprobed. They tend to be dishonest because their cleverness often enables them to 'get away with it'. They change opinions and swop principles if it will further their interests, and their love of ferreting turns them into gossips and intriguers. They are very shallow. Their mental agility makes them argumentative and fidgety and they are rarely generous unless it will benefit them in some way.

Well-Known Gemini Natives
Lord Thomson, Sir Laurence Olivier, John Masefield, Igor Stravinsky, Francoise Sagan, Field Marshal Earl Haig, Sir Frank Whittle, Elias Ashmole, Alexander

Pope, Queen Victoria, William Pitt, Thomas Moore (poet), Peter the Great, George Stephenson, Charles Kingsley, John Wesley, Pascal, Queen Mary, Sir John Cockcroft, Lord Parker, Lord Gardiner, Duke of Norfolk, George V, Arthur Ransome, George III, Captain R. F. Scott, Pietro Annigoni, Duke of Edinburgh (Prince Philip), Earl of Avon, W. B. Yeats, J. L. Baird, Henry Kissinger, Field Marshall Sir Claude Auchinleck, Bertrand Russell, Enoch Powell.

Cancer the Crab ♋ 22 June-22 July: *Water Sign*.

Good Cancer: Sentimental in the best sense of the word; that is, strongly attached to home, family and country. Make stout friends and allies who stand by one in adversity. They prefer the established order and traditions and dislike change. Kind, tolerant, modest and home-loving; excellent housewives, mothers and nurses and, naturally, neat, clean and methodical. They are prominent in good causes and have a strong sympathy for the under-dog; as a result, honest if they go into politics. They are romantic. Make good managers of hotels, inns and cafes, for they give sound value for money and they excel in all businesses where liquids are concerned: distilleries, breweries, water-works, oil refineries.

Bad Cancer: Sentimentality degenerates into un-balanced vanity. Imagination makes them a prey to flatterers. Unstable and unreliable. They lack the moral fibre of the good Cancer subject and when up against it indulge in self pity. Hypersensitive, which gives them an inferiority complex and makes them put on a show of over-confidence. Lazy, negative and diffident when it comes to asserting themselves.

Well-Known Cancer Natives
John Churchill, first Duke of Marlborough, Leibnitz,

Henry VIII, Dumas, Danilo Dolci, Marc Chagall, Serge Voronoff, Illya Metchnikov, Sir William Blackstone, John Hunter, Joshua Reynolds, Dr John Dee, Sir Julian Huxley, Helen Keller, Sir Alec Douglas-Home, Henry Cabot Lodge, Edward Heath, A. J. Cronin, Jack Dempsey, Oscar Hammerstein, Ginger Rogers, Gina Lollobrigida, Cyril Smith.

Leo the Lion ♌ 23 July-22 August: *Fire Sign*.

Good Leo: This type has all the qualities associated with the noble beast: courageous, bold in action and thought, open. They say what they think without hedging. You know on which side of the fence they stand. Frankness is accompanied by kindness and optimism for they radiate confidence, put their hearts into any enterprise they start, and love to lead, organize and command. Leos are eminently fitted for positions of authority or in which they can assert themselves: in the armed forces, at the heads of commercial and industrial concerns; as top Civil Servants. Their very nature fits them for posts as diplomats, ambassadors, and vice-chancellors of universities.

Bad Leo: Boldness, courage and determination are diverted into the wrong channels and they degenerate into dictators, becoming arrogant, ruthless, vain and boastful. They hate taking second place and try to lead whether they have the ability or not, thus often failing. They love to show off and they are pompous and touchy. Can't bear to be crossed, so great is their vanity.

Well-Known Leo Natives
George Bernard Shaw, Princess Margaret Rose, Mrs Onassis (Jacqueline Kennedy), Queen Elizabeth (wife of George VI), John Hay Witney, Percy Bysshe Shelley, Izaak Walton, John Dryden, Thomas Telford, Robert Southey, Lavoisier, Napoleon, Sir Walter Scott, Thomas

de Quincey, Prime Minister Earl Russell, Flamsteed, James Nasmyth, Selwyn Lloyd, Jo Grimond, Henry Moore, Sir Arthur Bliss, Sir Granville Bantock, Sir Basil Spence, John Galsworthy, Princess Anne, Sir Walter Scott.

Virgo the Virgin ♍ 23 August-23 September: *Earth Sign.*

Good Virgo: This is the sign of intellect and all who come under its influence are thorough, methodical, painstaking, industrious and able to master the intricacies of any subject or problem they care to tackle. The easiest to educate because they love to learn; and they like to give good service. Endowed with a sense of logic and responsibility, the ability to think clearly, argue and organize, they make capable writers, lecturers, debaters and scientists. As their clarity of thought is unequalled they excel in all branches of the written and spoken word.

Bad Virgo: Their love of learning is apt to make them pedantic, dislike correction, and they become so absorbed with detail that the general picture becomes blurred. They suspect everything and go to extremes of scepticism, becoming both hypercritical and hypocritical. They are the narrow-minded bores of this world, indulge in sarcasm and arouse the dislike of most people. They are mean with money. Many degenerate into misers and recluses because they feel that the world is antagonistic towards them, whereas in fact, they are the victims of their own pettiness and intolerance.

Well-Known Virgo Natives
H. G. Wells, J. B. Priestley, Leonard Bernstein, John Dalton, Robert Walpole, Prince Albert, John Locke, Caligula, John Howard, Matthew Boulton, Richelieu, Elizabeth I, Buffon, Samuel Johnson, Mungo Park, Von Humboldt, John Fenimore Cooper, Condorcet,

Alexander the Great, Macadam, Roy Walensky, Greta Garbo, Sophia Loren, Rocky Marciano, President Johnson, Sir Bernard Lovell, Mark Phillips, Edith Sitwell, Twiggy, Lady Antonia Fraser.

Libra the Scales ♎ 24 September-23 October: *Air Sign*.
Good Libra: The glyph represents a pair of scales denoting that the native has a singularly balanced, harmonious nature, can see both sides of any problem and will go to *almost* any lengths to avoid friction; but if in the right he will fight to the death for his principles. Easy to get on with and physically well proportioned and graceful. Appreciative of the arts and beauty in general; well-mannered and cheerful; modest, patient, idealistic. Librans usually do well in all the arts, make graceful dancers, superb diplomats, and because of their innate sense of justice, good lawyers.
Bad Libra: The playboys of this world. Though they have artistic gifts they are too lazy to study and work, so rarely achieve anything. Their main failing is vanity; they are flamboyant, garrulous, untidy and lack taste. They are endowed with plenty of superficial charm and spend much time in flirtations. They lack backbone and take the line of least resistance and instead of making friends create enemies through conceit, thoughtlessness, frivolity and self-indulgence. More than natives of any other sign they crave the approbation of the world, but because of their disinclination for solid work, rarely earn it.

Well-Known Libra Natives
Pope Paul VI, William Faulkner, Sir A. P. Herbert, Graham Greene, Lord Hailsham, Eamon de Valera, Dwight D. Eisenhower, Horatio Nelson, Mahatma Gandhi, George Gershwin, Marshal Foch, Ramsey MacDonald, Nicholas Culpeper, E. Phillips

Oppenheim, Jenny Lind, Archbishop Laud, Cervantes, Henry Cavendish, William Penn, Beau Nash, Sir Thomas Browne, Leigh Hunt, Jonathan Swift, Christopher Wren, Lord Clive, Julie Andrews, Bridgette Bardot, Trevor Howard, Harold Pinter, Margaret Thatcher, Jimmy Carter, P. G. Wodehouse, Annie Besant.

Scorpio the Scorpion ♏ 24 October-22 November: *Water Sign*.

Good Scorpio: Determined, tenacious, courageous, decisive, aggressive. This type thinks clearly, is energetic and likes to dominate but not subjugate. Scorpios have personal magnetism and often throw out a healing force. Reliable, honest, logical, observant, thorough; but secretive with strong native caution. Because they are ready to accept responsibilities one often sees them at the head of affairs. Usually they enjoy robust health. Successful in many walks of life but specially fitted to be doctors, surgeons, scientists, soldiers, teachers, sportsmen and engage in professions connected with liquids, oil, wine, etc.

Bad Scorpio: Perhaps the worst of the twelve signs, because determination changes to obstinacy, aggression to bullying and oppression; decisiveness to ruthlessness. Some of the cruellest, most fanatical men in history have come under this sign. They pick quarrels easily for the sake of stirring up trouble and grow suspicious, jealous and mean. They are the most jealous of all types, think and speak evilly of others and are extremely vindictive. Their speech is sarcastic and they browbeat those incapable of standing up for themselves. More often than not they bring about their own downfall. Goebbels was typical of this type.

Well-Known Scorpio Natives
Richard Burton, Katherine Hepburn, Vivien Leigh,

Joan Sutherland, Grace Kelly, Field Marshal
Montgomery, Field Marshal Rommel, Charles de
Gaulle, Jacob Epstein, Danton, Captain James Cook,
Edmund Halley, Boswell, Sheridan, John Evelyn,
Herschel, Mohammed, Martin Luther, Oliver
Goldsmith, Andrew Marvell, Picasso, Edward VII,
Prince Charles, Roy Jenkins, Charles I, Harold
Nicholson, Edmund Blunden, Nehru, Mrs Indira
Gandhi, Cowper, J. B. S. Haldane, John Keats, R. B.
Sheridan, James Cook, Hogarth, George Eliot.

Sagittarius the Archer ♐ 23 November-20 December:
Fire Sign.

   Good Sagittarius: Extroverts who love life and show
it. Nature and animal lovers who live in the country for
preference or escape to it when they can. Confident,
open, optimistic, impulsive, with a cheerful outlook on
life. They take a broad view of things and are extremely
tolerant; because of this, usually wise. Have excellent
judgment. They love travel and many explorers have
the sign prominent in their charts. Positive in outlook;
revel in life; productive. They make fine athletes,
hunters, travellers, wholesale merchants, bankers,
executive Civil Servants, judges and magistrates.

   Bad Sagittarius: Being extroverts by nature, the
natives tend to grow boastful, arrogant, dishonest and
untruthful. Not only do they lack tact but are often
hurtful and thoughtless. Spendthrift by nature and easily
taken in; instead of developing a justifiable confidence
they think they know everything and talk and exaggerate
too much. Love being in the limelight, swagger and put
on an act, but there is little behind the facade of show.
Always trying to impress.

Well-Known Sagittarius Natives
Winston Churchill, Spinoza, Louise Alcott, Sir Leslie
Stephen, Warren Hastings, Berlioz, Sir Philip Sidney,

Swift, Samuel Crompton, Carlyle, Milton, Gustave Adolphus, Admiral Hood, Tycho Brahe, Romney, Jane Austen, Weber, Beethoven, Sir Humphry Davy, Sir Edward Parry, Thomas à Becket, Lord Devlin, Queen Alexandra, Sir Osbert Sitwell, Lord Butler, King George VI, Noël Coward, Prince William, Sir Robert Menzies, Frank Sinatra, Maria Callas, Ian Botham, Solzhenitsyn.

Capricorn the Goat ♑ 21 December-19 January: *Earth Sign*.

Good Capricorn: Under this sign we find the plodders of the world; hard-working, utterly reliable servants; extremely ambitious for authority, a position in the world and the accumulation of wealth, property — all accomplished by patient effort. They are meticulous, love accuracy, think deeply and with intense concentration, and cling to old customs, habits, traditions and ways. They dislike too much change and have a keen sense of duty which makes them admirable politicians and government servants. They are at home in institutions where the routine is regular and the inmates hedged in by rules and regulations. Cautious like the goat, they dislike moving till sure of a foundation. They have considerable self-control, like solitude and can keep secrets. Their love of accuracy fits them for every branch of engineering except mining, and for agriculture. They love the earth but also excel in philosophy and do well in management. Hard taskmasters.

Bad Capricorn: Depressing people, always seeing the black side of life or of problems, and determined that they can't be solved. They worry too much about appearances, like to show a good front to the world and are always niggling. Affected badly by moods and tend to exist in the past. Narrow-minded, mean, greedy for wealth and possessions, miserly, bitter, envious, inflexible. Unhappy people.

Well-Known Capricorn Natives

Pablo Casals, Aristotle Onassis, Carl Sandburg, Albert Schweitzer, Neville Shute, Galina Ulanova, Richard Nixon, Kipling, Porson, Newton, Richard Arkwright, Compton Mackenzie, Romney, Gladstone, Edmund Burke, General Wolfe, Joan d'Arc, Benjamin Franklin, Charles James Fox, Montesquieu, James Watt, J. Edgar Hoover, John Crome, Sir Michael Tippett, Earl Attlee, Marlene Dietrich, Cezanne.

Aquarius the Water Bearer ≈ 20 January-19 February: *Air Sign*.

Good Aquarius: Tolerant, likeable, easygoing, quick in thought and action, witty and creative. The native is intelligent, often intellectual; independent, progressive in outlook, full of enthusiasm and loves travel. The great reformers have Aquarius strong in their charts. They love taking up causes and often lead movements and reforms, unfortunately to the neglect of their families. They try to improve humanity but frequently beggar themselves in the process. The new and novel attracts them and they are exciting people to have around. Make good technicians and inventors. Radio, TV, computers and inter-continental travel are tailor-made for them. Their quickness and flexibility of mind makes them good actors and writers, but journalists rather than writers of serious works.

Bad Aquarius: Disorganized people whose affairs are forever in a mess. They are erratic and fall easily under the influence of stronger wills; unreliable and over-enthusiastic. The men tend to be effeminate; the women cold. Both sexes are neurotic, psychosomatic and lacking in self-control. They associate with Bohemians, take easily to drugs and end without aim or purpose in life. Well-meaning but weak and vacillating.

Well-Known Aquarius Natives

Ronald Reagan, Tallulah Bankhead, Adlai Stevenson, Charles Lindberg, Colette, Harold Macmillan, Charles Lamb, Francis Galton, Franklin D. Roosevelt, the famous Piccard twins, Mozart, Abraham Lincoln, Francis Bacon, Byron, Burns, Swedenborg, Tom Paine, Ben Jonson, Sir Robert Peel, Dickens, Congreve, Galileo, Copernicus, Lord Denning, Cardinal Heenan, Sir Stanley Matthews, Dean Rusk, Lord Franks, Prince Andrew.

Pisces the Fishes ✕ 20 February-20 March: *Water Sign*.

Good Pisces: Kind, helpful, peace loving and self sacrificing. Receptive to the woes of others and sensitive enough to feel the wrongs done to them. They spend their lives working for or sponsoring good causes without expecting rewards, so make excellent missionaries and members of voluntary charity organizations. Idealistic, warm hearted, generous, sympathetic and full of under-standing. More often than not, misunderstood. Imbued with strong religious feeling and usually psychic to some degree. Saints have a strong Pisces strain and it is probable that Christ was born under this sign and not in December. They gravitate towards psychology, the priesthood, chemistry and the more sober branches of the arts. The world would be poorer without the good Pisces.

Bad Pisces: Indecision afflicts this type, who find it impossible to make up their minds and take a firm stand. They have an inbred guilt complex, become moody and sometimes seek martydom. Their sensitive natures make them unduly touchy and as they are unable to express themselves lucidly are usually misunderstood. They become secretive, hypocritical and take to intrigue, drink, masochism or religion. As they are willing to believe almost anything they often become hysterical.

The most unstable of all types.

Well-Known Piscean Natives

Georgios S. Sepheriades and Giulio Natta (Nobel Prize winners), Einstein, John Steinbeck, Neville Chamberlain, Bentham, Montaigne, Pepys, Newcomb and Schiaparelli (astronomers), Kenneth Grahame, David Garrick, George Washington, Handel, Hugo, Longfellow, William Cobbett, William Etty, Berkeley, Harold Wilson, Lord Snowdon (A. Armstrong-Jones), Cardinal Newman, W. H. Auden, George Washington, Ronald Searle, David Niven, Patty Hearst, Yuri Gagarin, Maxim Gorky, Viscount Chandos.

Physical Characteristics

When we speak of a person being 'under a sign', we mean that the sign was in his Sun at the day and hour of birth and he will be influenced by it mentally and physically. We have already outlined the mental attributes of those under the various signs; here then, are the physical characteristics.

Aries: ♈ Lean torso and slim neck, prominent cheek bones, and light brown hair, either wiry or crisp and curly. Front teeth usually large or prominent. You will, of course, come across many Aries people who do not bear out this description, but do not write astrology off as nonsense. There will probably be other signs in the chart which bear even more strongly on him, and will modify his appearance considerably. Only if he is a 'true' Aries will he bear out this description entirely. And that applies, of course, to all other types.

Taurus: ♉ Solid, thick-set, bull-necked, with powerful shoulders topped by a bullet head. Brown eyes, full lips, dark wavy hair. Hands full and fleshy, and feet, too, though these are usually encased in shoes.

Gemini: ♊ Taller than average, straight-backed and

active. Wide, thin lips, straight or up-tilted nose, wide shoulders with flattish chest; straight dark hair.

Cancer: ♋ Short and dumpy, with active lymphatic glands which produce a pallor. Moon face, wide forehead, large liquid eyes and indeterminate brown hair. Chest in keeping with the figure, full and deep; soft, fleshy hands.

Leo: ♌ Well above average height, with fine athletic figure, well proportioned head; often blonde or with light brown hair. Very open appearance.

Virgo: ♍ Wiry, with broad forehead, well proportioned head topped with light brown hair, blue eyes. Shoulders broad in proportion to the rest of the body.

Libra: ♎ Well developed, graceful and even elegant; blue or brown eyes; brown or light brown hair with a glint in it and a fine skin. The pure Libran is the most attractive type.

Scorpio: ♏ Short, sturdy, powerful, with barrel chest and swarthy or sallow complexion. Hair crisp and rough; legs bowed and strong. Physically and constitutionally tough.

Sagittarius: ♐ Tall, well proportioned, athletic; oval face usually rather long, surmounted by brown hair. Expressive eyes, usually dark brown or blue; nose somewhat longer than usual — often aquiline.

Capricorn: ♑ Slighter build than normal with scraggy neck and prominent Adam's apple. A narrow chin makes the features seem larger and more prominent — especially the nose — and the face stern. Weak chest with sloping shoulders. The pure Capricorn is perhaps the least attractive type.

Aquarius: ♒ Tall, well-formed and pleasing; regular features, a good skin, determined chin and wide brow. Usually fair with blue eyes.

Pisces: ♓ Usually under average height with limbs in proportion. Pale skin, short nose, often turned up, round face and fleshly lips. Eyes large and liquid with the ends of the mouth turned down. Plump hands.

True Taurus, Cancer, Capricorn and Pisces types are under average height; Gemini, Leo, Sagittarius and Aquarius are above average height; the remainder are medium height.

In speaking about blue eyes, blonde complexion and fair hair one must bear in mind that these refer to Europeans and North Americans. In judging Asians and Africans these directions should be disregarded, but bodily indications such as height, fleshiness and eye-shape, apply to all races.

- Millions are not, of course, absolutely true to type, but are powerfully influenced by other signs. As you master the subject you will see how these influences work to produce the types they do, and why different types will act differently when confronted with the same problems and situations. Astrology is a fascinating study and the real key to psychology and healing.

CHAPTER THREE

WHAT THE PLANETS MEAN

When we say that our destiny lies in the stars we do not speak accurately because except for the Sun, Moon and the planets, the stars in our universe affect us not at all; and there are millions of them. But the planets, which move at a constant distance from the earth at any given time and have regular, fixed courses, do.

These bodies comprise an infinitesimal portion of our universe and we have learnt within recent years that ours

is only one of many universes, and an insignificant one
at that. None of these millions of stars directly affect our
earth or the people on it.

The Sun ☉

The rays of the sun warm us and produce the energy
which gives life to everything in the animal and vegetable
kingdom and endows minerals with certain properties
and powers. If coal is ignited, for instance, power is
released in the form of heat. Inside masses of pitch-blende
lie microscopic quantities of uranium, which produce
atomic power. We can see and feel the influence of the
sun, and acknowledge it. It is significant that the
Persians, Incas, Aztecs and the Ancient Greeks and
Egyptians worshipped the sun; and the Zoroastrians face
it when they pray.

In astrology all that is high and powerful comes under
the rule of the sun: emperors, kings, popes, political
leaders such as prime ministers (dictators come under
the rule of Uranus) come under the sun. And in less
elevated spheres the sun denotes your own personality
in a horoscope; or that of the father of a family; or the
husband in a woman's horoscope. The sun represents
the grand, the royal, and the important. It rules gold.

The Moon ☽

The Moon, though having no light of its own, throws
off reflected power from the sun, which affects many on
this earth when it is full. The word *lunatic* is derived from
the Latin *luna*, moon, and any doctor or nurse in an
asylum for the insane will tell you that some of the inmates
grow violent when the moon is full. Humans in the
tropics, where moonlight is far more intense than in
Britain, are apt to get moonstruck if they sleep under
the moon, and certain fish become poisonous if the moon
is allowed to play on them after they have been caught.

Sleeping animals invariably move from moonlight into the shade.

We know that tides all over the world are caused by the attraction of the moon and that water, even in wells far inland, rises and falls as the moon waxes and wanes. Plants are also affected and their growth can be stimulated if seeds are sown before or just after full-moon, depending on their type.

Experiences over scores of centuries have shown that the moon affects the emotions. The ancients planted according to the moon and mated their flocks to coincide with its rising; it is associated in astrology with conception, fertility, human feelings, population, and mass movements.

In the horoscope of a woman the moon represents her personality; in that of a man, it points to the woman or women in his life — mother, sister, wife, friend — who have influenced him. As the moon is constantly changing, it denotes changes, emotions, enthusiasms, depression and elation.

Not without reason, the moon has always been associated with women; and this applies in the horoscope. Receptive and intuitive people, such as psychics, are said to have 'a strong moon influence', and no one can be an artist without having the moon strongly aspected in more than one position. As the moon is a feminine influence, all good artists have a distinct streak of the feminine in their composition. This doesn't mean that they are 'cissies', but that they feel more powerfully than other people and that is why they are inspired by sounds, colours and situations that leave normal people unmoved. The moon rules silver and represents movement.

Mercury ☿

In astrological lore the planet Mercury represents the

mind, reason, intelligence, intellect, purpose, aim. It stands for trade, commerce, industry and travel — any travel, provided it has a purpose. It deals with the world of the mind and embraces all forms of literature, writing and the expression of thoughts and ideas. It rules the mineral mercury (quicksilver), which runs, flows and darts unpredictably and is difficult to cage.

Venus ♀

The Ancient Greeks called Venus the God of Love and Beauty and this is what the planet symbolizes in astrology: love, universal harmony, and beauty. All that is elegant, picturesque, attractive and sympathetic comes under Venus; the entire world of fashion, cosmetics and music; the singer and the musician, but not the composer. The mineral associated with Venus is copper.

Mars ♂

In classical lore Mars was the God of War. In astrology this planet stands for energy and the power of will; all forms of violent movement and activity, whether peaceful as in sport and athletics, or warlike. It governs force of every kind: soldiers, armaments, attack, defence, destruction. The police and the fire service which are organized for the benefit of humanity, come under Mars. Naturally, the mineral associated with Mars is iron, from which steel is made and weapons of war fashioned.

Jupiter ♃

Since the dawn of civilization Jupiter has been the God that rules law and wisdom, so in astrology it has become the symbol of authority: judges, vice-chancellors of universities, principals of colleges and schools; high officials of every kind — professors, lecturers, teachers. It also rules the world of knowledge and science; and because it symbolizes Justice, sport and fair play. 'It isn't

cricket', is a typical Jupiterian observation. The mineral
ruled by Jupiter is tin, which in its pure state is more
costly than silver.

Saturn ♄

Saturn represents all that is old, traditional, unchanging,
inflexible and negative. It is the symbol of materialism,
old age, obstacles, tribulations, handicaps, misfortune
and enmity; not quick, surging, rushing anger that flares
up and dies quickly, but the slow burning type of enmity
that lasts till death. Generally speaking it is an
unfortunate symbol reflecting poverty, oppression,
slavery, despotism, greed, sullen hate and sterility. It
has close associations with the old — those older than
the native; on occasion with ancestors. Saturn has a
retarding effect, which sometimes is needed. Its metal
is lead: ugly, heavy, dull.

Uranus ♅

Uranus was not discovered till 1781 and its influence
determined by observation and experiment. It symbolizes upheaval, revolution, invention, change and tension.
All these tend more often than not in some way to
catastrophe. Even the best of inventions have brought
misery and disaster in their train. It is symbolic of the
unconventional and the revolutionary; but also of
original minds, and perverts. The world of the cinema,
radio, television, computers, atomic science, interplanetary travel and airplanes come under Uranus; so
do earthquakes, explosions and upheavals; any sudden
change, in fact, that upsets the established order. The
mineral associated with Uranus is aluminium, which
was discovered just over 100 years ago.

Neptune ♆

Neptune was discovered in 1846, but this does not

invalidate the accuracy of astrology. Neptune represents the higher mind; spiritual healing, mysticism and chaos. It symbolizes the nebulous; imagination, intuition, fantasy, as well as spiritual dishonesty. It also represents dishonesty in material matters. The seemingly formless, chaotic music of the ultra-moderns is a Neptunian trend; so is the addiction to drugs which produce visions and hallucinations. Other Neptunian tendencies are: a tendency to probe industrial and military secrets and the wave towards idealism, unchannelled and unconstructive as it seems to be.

Neptunian influence seems strong in the hysterical desire for a Utopia, and the way in which mob hysteria seems to dominate the world. Neptune seems to signify idealism that somehow has lost its direction and ended in chaos and anarchy.

CHAPTER FOUR

THE HOUSES

We now know something about the Signs and the Planets, what they symbolize and represent. Let us now take a look at the Houses.

No measurement has, or can be, made of our Universe, so no one knows how vast it is or where the centre stands. For purposes of astrology the native whose horoscope is being charted is the centre, at the place and moment of birth. This is an arbitrary definition of 'centre' but works in practice.

In actual fact the earth moves around the sun but for the sake of convenience we speak, for instance, of the sun 'moving into the sign of Aries', or into the First House, or the Tenth House, as the case may be. In practice the earth has revolved in such a way that the Sign of Aries has become powerfully influenced by the sun.

For the purpose of astrology, that limited area of the heavens known as the Zodiac is divided into twelve equal sections, each of 30 degrees.

The astrological year does not start on New Year's Day but on 21 March, when the sun is at the Vernal Equinox, and in astrological parlance 'the sun enters Aries'.

Anyone born in the middle of the Sign; that is, from 28 March-13 April, will be a much more characteristic Aries subject than if born nearer to 21 March or 20 April, in which case he is liable to be affected either by Pisces, the sign before Aries, or Taurus, the sign following Aries.

First House
This house represents YOU; your character, personality, and individuality. It conveys some idea of your physical appearance; the way you walk, talk, think and hold yourself. It is the house of your character.

Second House
This is your money house. A study of it will provide a picture of your financial affairs at any given period; your possessions and your ability to handle them. It embraces everything dealing with income, either profit or loss, but not with inheritance.

Third House
The third house encompasses three distinct aspects of your life: relatives; writing and correspondence; travel. Your dealings with brothers, sisters, cousins and aunts will be shown here. It is also the house of the mind and

interests connected with the mind; writers, for instance, have indications which show this. Finally, travel; journeys long and short, especially those concerned with your work or education. If you travel more than a thousands miles to school, as I did, this will be shown in the third house.

Fourth House

Here we are given information about your close ancestors and how they have affected your life; your relations with your parents and their influence. Here will be shown whether you've had early hardships or were brought up in comfort or luxury; whether you enjoyed a stable, established homelife, or one that was broken by changes and travel, or shattered by divorce.

This house shows whether you have landed possessions or houses. It also gives indications about the second half of your life, usually the most important half; and a glimpse of circumstances at the end of life.

Fifth House

This is the house of Love, Luck and Life. It is possible from a study of the planets in this house at the time of birth, to estimate the degree of your sexual impulses; whether you will be amorous, cold, normal or perverted. Because of this, people born with quirks should not be judged too harshly. This house shows how many children you will have. It encompasses sport, hobbies, art, amusements of every kind — even betting, gambling and speculation. Your personal popularity is mirrored here.

Sixth House

There are two main divisions here, of which health is perhaps the more important, for if one has robust health almost any setbacks can be faced with equanimity. The

diseases likely to afflict you are outlined — also
operations. It will be shown whether your constitution
is sound, and whether you will be fat or thin. It indicates
the type of food you should eat.

The second division gives a picture of your relations
with inferiors; that is, if you occupy a position of authority
or have inherited position, wealth and honours. If you
are an employee or occupy an inferior position, your
prospects will be shown.

Seventh House
This is the house in which most women are keenly
interested because it deals with marriage and partnerships, both marital and business. Will you and your
spouse live in amity; will you part, be divorced, or left
a widow; will your partner be good for you, or bad? All
this is indicated. Also, the way in which the world in
general reacts towards you; whether you will be a social
success, or enter into business or political partnerships.
You will be warned of dangers in such connections, and
advised to take advantage of chances.

Eighth House
Generally known as the house of death, for it gives
indications of the *probable* method of your passing, but
not the precise time. You may be blown up, drowned,
or die unexcitingly in bed, and the possibility is shown.
There are many permutations to be worked out and here
the skill of the astrologer is all-important. This house
tells of inheritance and warns of dangers and benefits,
for money and possession don't invariably make for
happiness.

It also deals with the psychic.

Ninth House
This is the house of the higher mind: religion, philosophy

and all that is concerned with them: agnosticism, fanaticism, faith, missionary enterprises. Here will be effectively exposed the hypocrite who wears the cloak of piety.

Long journeys, especially foreign travel, are shown; their purpose, influence on the native, and their outcome. You will see from a study of this house whether you are likely to live in the land of your birth, or emigrate and die abroad.

Tenth House
The house of career. As the profession or professions for which you are suited are outlined here, this is of paramount importance to parents, especially those who have already decided that John must follow in the footsteps of his father, who has built up and established a prosperous business. But if John has no aptitude for the work the business may lie in ruins a couple of years after his father's death. Parents are shown what their children can do, and what they are best fitted for.

The sense of duty, or lack of it, is also shown, and indications of power, position and honours.

Eleventh House
You are told about your friends and the types that will benefit you, and those that will do you harm or lead you astray. Your hopes, desires, wishes, ambitions, and possible fulfilment, are also shown. Useful information, indeed.

Twelfth House
It is good to know your enemies and be warned about them. These are shown here, and you are shown what sort of people they are.

Some ruin themselves by being involved in law suits; this house will show whether you are likely to win or lose.

It will also show whether you will be closely connected with charitable institutions, hospitals or jails; whether you will be an official or an inmate. In this house you will see the death of others, either near to you or who concern you in some way.

Now we know the Signs and what they mean; the Planets and what they represent; the Houses and what they hold in store for you.

The Signs at the moment of birth indicate the type of person you are. The transit or travel of the Planets through the various Houses will indicate your varying fortunes from day to day; even from hour to hour, for the horoscope is neither constant nor stationary. By studying these movements it is possible to say what will happen to the native in business, marriage or any other sphere of life, now in the future. You will get a picture of possible success or disaster, or of nothing in particular. If of disaster, steps can be taken to ameliorate the worst or nullify the damage; or even so to act that disaster, when it comes, can be turned to one's advantage, as sometimes happens.

The Aspects

The Aspects are angular distances between the Planets and are measured by the angle made between a line drawn from one planet to the centre of the earth, and a line from there to another planet. Thus, if the sun is at right angles to the moon we say that it is 'in square' aspect with the moon. If they are 120° apart, they are 'in trine', and if 180°, 'in opposition'. The aspects generally used are:

☌	Conjunction		Variable
⊻	Semi-sextile	30°	Weak harmony
∠	Semi-square	45°	Weak discord
⚹	Sextile	60°	Harmony, good

□	Square	90°	Discord; bad
△	Trine	120°	Harmony, very good
⊡	Sesquiquadrate	135°	Weak, discord
⊼	Quincunx	150°	Weak, discord
⚹	Opposition	180°	Discord, bad
P	Parallel		Variable

Conjunction: ♂ if two planets are in the same place or within five degrees of each other they are said to be 'in conjunction'; or even if they are not in the same place, but adjacent. Where conjunctions occur you will have to exercise judgement. If Saturn and Mars are 'in conjunction' or 'conjunct', the result will not be good because these are what is known as 'malefic planets'. If on the other hand, Jupiter and Venus are conjunct the effect will not only be very good, but powerful.

Aspects are really strong only when *in conjunction, sextile, square, trine,* and *in opposition*.

In practice, don't write the aspects in words; always use the symbols, and very quickly you will become conversant with them. They are the shorthand of astrology.

Orbs

The effects of the planets are felt not only when they are precisely in aspect but also a little before and a little after, and the angle of effect is known as the *Orb* (Latin: *orbis*, circle). This differs for different planets and there is some disagreement among astrologers as to the distance away that the effects of orbs are felt. Some say that aspects involving the sun and moon have an orb of 10-12 degrees before and after coming into aspect — during which their influences are felt. For aspects involving Jupiter, Saturn, Uranus and Neptune, the angle will be about 8 degrees; and for Mars, Venus and Mercury, as little as 6 degrees.

One of the great modern astrologers, Sepharial

(Walter Gorn Old) says: 'The orbs of the planets are of the following dimensions, within which radius they are capable of acting as if in conjunction: the Sun 15, Moon 12, Jupiter 10, Saturn 9, Venus 8, Mars 7, Mercury, Uranus and Neptune 5 each. Thus if the Sun were in Aries 1 and Uranus in Aries 16, the Sun would be within Orbs of Uranus'.

You will discover as you dig deeper into the study of astrology that many eminent astrologers differ in method and degree, but when all is said and done, the results are virtually the same.

The influences will be far more potent if the aspects are precisely the same but when within orbs it will be left to your judgement to decide. It is here that the human element enters, and a dozen charts worked out by a dozen astrologers, of the same person, may all differ in minor respects, but give the same over-all picture.

CHAPTER FIVE

THE INFLUENCE OF THE PLANETS (ASPECTS)

Ruling Planets
In astrology we talk about signs being ruled by certain planets. By this we mean that there is a powerful affinity between them, as for instance:

Aries and Scorpio
These signs are ruled by the planet Mars. Turn back to the chapter on the signs and you will see that both types are fiery, energetic, possess plenty of initiative and have a tendency to be bellicose. They are the doers and adventurers.

Now refresh your memory by turning to the section

on the planets and you will find that Mars, the God of War, is symbolic of courage, activity, passion, force. It stimulates and energizes. It is obvious that there must be a strong affinity between the planet Mars and these two signs, so in astrological terms we say that 'Mars rules Aries and Scorpio'.

Taurus and Libra
Likewise, Taurus and Libra are ruled by Venus. Turn back and read about these signs and then about Venus and once again you will find that there exists much in common.

Gemini and Virgo
Gemini and Virgo are strong mental signs. Those who come under them are noted for their mental agility — even intellect. They learn and speak easily and fluently and are changeable and volatile. Mercury represents the reasoning faculties and rational man; intelligence, the world of writing, so it will be seen that there is a strong compatability.

Cancer
The Cancer native is sentimental, emotional, home-loving, etc.; it is fitting therefore that Cancer should be ruled by the moon, which symbolizes the emotional life, romantic and intuitive.

Leo
The Leo native is warm, open, expansive, enterprising, noble in outlook; all the attributes represented by the sun, which is its ruler.

Sagittarius and Pisces
Sagittarius and Pisces are ruled by Jupiter, which, as you know, represents law and order and authority;

equity; sport and games, so it is natural that Jupiter should rule Sagittarius. Pisces, however, is only partly ruled by Jupiter and this is apparent by the readiness of Pisceans, who go in for good works and humanitarian enterprises, to accept their destiny. Pisces has, however, another ruler in Neptune, which represents spirituality, dreaminess, mysticism and chaos, which is more in keeping with the character of Pisces.

Capricorn

Saturn is the ruler of Capricorn, and if you examine the characteristics of Capricorn and compare them with those of Saturn you will find much in common: industriousness, serious mindedness, caution, love of duty of Capricorn and the hindrance, hardship, obstacles, adherence to old traditions and dislike of change symbolized by Saturn.

Aquarius

Aquarius has dual rulership, as well: Saturn and Uranus, and of the two Uranus seems more in keeping with the sign, with its emphasis on change, especially abrupt change. Here Saturn has a good, modifying influence, lending balance to the nature.

When a planet comes into a sign it influences it considerably, the exact degree depending on many factors, and here again it is the skill, knowledge and experience of the interpreter that matters. Nothing is cut and dried. The good astrologer has the ability to sift the informtion at his disposal and arrive at the correct conclusions and, as in every art, the ability to do so comes by constant practice.

Now let us consider some of the aspects with which you will inevitably have to deal in translating a horoscope:

Sun Trine Moon: Sun Sextile Moon: ⊙ △ ☽ ; ⊙ ⚹ ☽

We know that the trine is very good, and the sextile good. But in what way?

The sun is the source of life and energy; power and spirituality. The moon symbolizes changes of mood, popularity, enthusiasms, depressions. Either of these aspects ensures that the native will be open, have unusual vitality, be popular, loyal in friendship and have an excellent chance of a successful life.

This will be only one of many aspects in his chart and there will be others to consider; some beneficial; others not so good or positively harmful. In deciding you will have to weigh one against the other, an exercise in which no one can help you. In interpreting the chart every astrologer is on his own and his reputation will depend on the skill with which he weighs up the different aspects, balances them against each other and arrives at a decision. In this respect he is like a doctor who is given a number of symptoms by a patient and has to decide which really matter and by what they are caused. He then carries out his own tests such as taking the pulse rate, sounding the heart, palpating the chest, examining the tongue, before he arrives at certain conclusions. His diagnosis will decide whether he is a good doctor; and there are bad doctors as well as bad astrologers, and in both arts, the bad predominate.

Sun in Conjunction with Moon: ⊙ ☌ ☽

This for short, is usually referred to as 'Sun conjunct Moon', and is an aspect which needs experience to decide because as stated earlier the planets need to be in exactly the same place for them to be in conjunction and a certain latitude is allowed between different planets. Generally speaking, allow ten degrees between sun and moon. This is a favourable aspect though the proximity of these planets will tend to make the native hypersensitive.

Sun Square Moon; Sun Opposition Moon: ☉ ☐ ☽; ☉ ☍ ☽

Squares and oppositions are unfavourable. Life will be cluttered by obstacles and frustrations and those in superior positions will hamper rather than help. The native will be thin-skinned and take offence easily, and throughout life women will guide and advise him with unsatisfactory results. A weak constitution provides a fertile ground for disease.

Sun in Conjunction with Mercury: ☉ ☌ ☿

Mercury influences the mind and reason, also travel. It follows, therefore, that if not less than three degrees apart, in which case the Mercury influence will be swamped by the sun, this is a fairly good aspect, and gives the native the ability to learn easily and express himself lucidly. He may, however, think too much of himself.

The sun will never be in bad aspect with Mercury as the angle between them is never more than 28° and the nearest unfavourable aspect is semi-square or 45°. At most these two can be almost semi-sextile, which is always fairly good.

Sun Trine Venus; Sun Sextile Venus: ☉ △ ♀; ☉ ✳ ♀

Venus symbolizes harmony, colour, brightness, beauty and embraces the world of art. The combination produces an artistic, pleasant, cheerful, sympathetic person; refined and cultured. Women will dress with taste; men will have a sense of distinction. Both sexes will be popular.

Sun in Conjunction with Venus: ☉ ☌ ♀

We can regard this as a favourable aspect provided the sun is not three degrees or nearer, in which case it is said to be 'combust' with Venus.

Sun Trine Mars; Sun Sextile Mars: ☉ △ ♂; ☉ ✳ ♂
Trines are very good; sextiles good and both produce favourable influences: initiative, vitality, energy, force. Comparatively few rise to the highest ranks in the armed forces without these aspects. The native will be frank, honest, blunt, and will not easily accept opposition. Health will be superb. Very fortunate.

Sun in Conjunction with Mars: ☉ ♂ ♂
The contiguity of these two forceful planets makes the native impulsive, brusque, rude, given to exaggeration and a tendency to override others. He will lack the ability to sit back and make decisions.

Sun Square Mars; Sun Opposition Mars: ☉ ☐ ♂; ☉ ☍ ♂
The worst in these two powerful planets is brought out. Energy, courage and vitality become corrupted into violence, bullying, bad temper and sudden rages. The native will be irascible and unreasonable and will go about with 'a chip on his shoulder'. He will quarrel and bicker with those above him. Endowed with abnormal energy, he uses it destructively, is difficult to get on with, and will have nothing to do with those who disagree with him.

Sun Trine Jupiter; Sun Sextile Jupiter: ☉ △ ♃; ☉ ✳ ♃
The sun is the leader; Jupiter represents wisdom, law and authority. It would be difficult to have better aspects, for the native will almost certainly reach a high position in his profession. Natural leaders have these aspects; honest and upright and at the same time kindly and helpful to those who serve under them. If in the Civil

Service such people tend to be honoured; scientists might
end as Fellows of the Royal Society or even Nobel Prize
Winners.

Sun in Conjunction with Jupiter: ☉ ☌ ♃

Despite the nearness of the planets this is regarded as
a favourable sign as each casts its favourable influence
on the native.

Sun Square Jupiter; Sun Opposition Jupiter: ☉ ☐ ♃; ☉ ☍ ♃

The fact that one has either a square or an opposition
to Jupiter does not damn the native at the start. Many
have risen to the highest positions with such aspects.
President Franklin D. Roosevelt had Jupiter square Sun
in his chart but it did not prevent him from becoming
President. But it handicapped him by paralysing his legs
and making life extremely difficult; but other aspects
tended to counteract these influences. One must examine
the chart as a whole and not only one or two aspects. Then
weigh one against the other before deciding. But without
modifying influences these unfavourable aspects indicate
that the native will be arrogant, constantly quibbling
with a tendency to resort to legal action, and a bad
employer.

Sun Trine Saturn; Sun Sextile Saturn: ☉ △ ♄; ☉ ⚹ ♄

'Ah — Saturn — it must be bad!' So the beginner jumps
to conclusions because Saturn represents obstacles,
handicaps, hardship, poverty, the slowing of progress
and all that we associate with failure; but it also represents
persistence, tenacity, patience and common sense. When
these are allied with the qualities that the sun represents
then all the bountiful gifts that she promises may
eventually result through hard work and concentrated
effort. But success will come in the second half of life

and probably be all the sweeter for that, for a mature person appreciates and can make better use of success than the young; for as Shaw so truthfully said: 'Youth is wasted on the young!' With these aspects health tends to improve after *forty* and character and personality develop. Success, when it comes, will not be spectacular but well earned and satisfying.

Sun in Conjunction with Saturn: ☉ ☌ ♄

Saturn so close to the sun casts her baleful influence on the native and tends to make the naturally optimistic depressed and feel unjustly treated. Nevertheless, he will be a good organizer and executive, though perhaps a trifle too ambitious, with sad results.

Sun Square Saturn; Sun Opposition Saturn: ☉ □ ♄; ☉ ☍ ♄

These unfavourable influences bring constant frustration; plans go wrong; payments are held up; some who owe money go bankrupt. The early part of life will be extremely difficult, chances few and superiors unhelpful. Here again, you must examine the entire chart, observe the signs into which these aspects fall and decide whether the native is likely to be strengthened or weakened by adversity; whether success or failure is probable. Remember, even the worst aspects do not invariably mean final disaster.

Sun Trine Uranus; Sun Sextile Uranus: ☉ △ ♅; ☉ ✳ ♅

Though Uranus represents catastrophe and drastic changes, in itself it is neither good nor bad; it also represents new ideas, progress, advancement. In good aspect with the sun it means a clear, active mind full of progressive ideas; fertile, inventive. Engineers, scientists, writers — especially of science fiction, detection or new

forms of writing; or artists who paint in a new *genre* —
have these aspects. They make for constructive
originality.

Sun in Conjunction with Uranus: ☉ ☌ ♅

In such close proximity Uranus gives the native new ideas
and the ability to put them into operation. The sun's
febrile influence tends to make him hypersensitive and
act somewhat impulsively.

Sun Square Uranus; Sun Opposition Uranus: ☉ □ ♅; ☉ ☌ ♅

Uranus provides new and inventive ideas but these unfavourable aspects fail to endow the native with the ability
to carry them out satisfactorily. If he is an inventor, for
instance, he will be dogged by failure because he fails
to think constructively. The native is jumpy, unconventional, rarely sticks at anything for long; is undisciplined,
dislikes authority; will love the new, not because it is
better but because it is a change. The many-times
divorced often have these aspects but without modifying
influences.

Sun Trine Neptune; Sun Sextile Neptune: ☉ △ ♆; ☉ ⚹ ♆

Neptune represents the higher mind, mysticism,
spirituality; even chaos. The sun brings out all the best
and wisest in his character and gives him an interest in
religion, philosophy and science — also a love of comfort
or luxury. If the sun is in an artistic sign, such as Libra
or Taurus he will veer towards music. These people 'have
a way with them'.

Sun in Conjunction with Neptune: ☉ ☌ ♆

A fairly good aspect — with reservations. There will be
an inclination towards the occult and the mysterious and

he will tend to be secretive. Should the sun fall in Pisces, Cancer, Scorpio or Aquarius he will probably be psychic.

Sun Square Neptune; Sun Opposition Neptune: ☉ □ ♆; ☉ ☍ ♆

The benefic influences of the sun are nullified and we find a tendency to indulge in narcotics and dabble in poisons; a hankering after visions; a desire to probe secrets; and mental and sexual aberrations.

Moon Trine Mercury; Moon Sextile Mercury: ☽ △ ☿; ☽ ✶ ☿

The finest qualities of the moon blended with those of Mercury make the native sharp-witted, clever and adept at languages, especially if the moon is in Aquarius, Gemini, Virgo or Libra. As both moon and Mercury favour change there is a probability of much travel.

Moon Square Mercury; Moon Opposition Mercury: ☽ □ ☿; ☽ ☍ ☿

The opposing influences make the native hypersensitive, indecisive and hysterical; they fill him with fear and worry and he starts enterprises that are never completed. He is fussy, pedantic, too-meticulous and mentally unreliable, and worries unduly about health.

Moon Trine Venus; Moon Sextile Venus; Moon in Conjunction with Venus: ☽ △ ☿; ☽ ✶ ♀; ☽ ☌ ♀

Either of these aspects produces a favourable blend, the moon giving an interest in the arts; Venus endowing the native with excellent taste, the graces, and sound judgement. If either planet is in Taurus, Gemini, Cancer, Virgo, Libra or Aquarius interest in the arts will be strong and practical and the chances of material and social success excellent.

Moon Square Venus; Moon Opposition Venus: ☽ □ ♀; ☽ ☍ ♀

These aspects produce a character who lacks ballast; slipshod, unwilling to complete an undertaking; inability to seize chances. Bad habits are all-too-easily formed and the native is fickle and liable to change his mind without logical reason.

Moon Trine Mars; Moon Sextile Mars: ☽ △ ♂; ☽ ✶ ♂

Mars endows the native with robust health which enables him to make tremendous efforts to forge ahead. The moon, which colours the emotions, makes for strong sympathies and also feelings of revulsion. Commonsense and initiative in business is marked. Such aspects also have a love for the outdoors and for sport.

Moon in Conjunction with Mars: ☽ ☌ ♂

Ruggedness of physique and constitution, especially if Mars is in Scorpio (which it rules), Aries or Capricorn. There is a tendency where force and emotion are combined to make the native rash and inclined to take risks.

Moon Square Mars; Moon Opposition Mars: ☽ □ ♂; ☽ ☍ ♂

Impulsiveness engendered by the lunar influence coupled with the fire and strength of Mars tend to make the native leap before looking. He is insolent, domineering, but courageous; he is boastful, a bully, spiteful, wasteful. Only firm, early discipline can remedy such tendencies.

Moon Trine Jupiter; Moon Sextile Jupiter: ☽ △ ♃; ☽ ✶ ♃

The Jupiter influence makes the native just and frank and paves the way for success; good lunar influences make a happy marriage highly probable; what is more, the wife (or husband) will help the partner advance professionally without the sacrifice of dignity or poise.

Moon Square Jupiter; Moon Opposition Jupiter: ☽ □ ♃; ☽ ☍ ♃

The moon's influence, instead of helping the native, will hamper and hinder, tempt him to speculate foolishly, and cause loss of money and reputation. The judgement that Jupiter gives becomes unsettled by the influence of the moon, so that choice of profession, friends and wife are bad; colours his judgement and leads to mistakes. He complains that no one understands him, his wife least of all!

Moon Trine Saturn; Moon Sextile Saturn: ☽ △ ♄; ☽ ✳ ♄

The moon charges the emotions and makes for change, but here oft-spurned Saturn provides stability and trust.

The native is loyal to wife, friends and business associates; his ventures are well planned and seen through to the end. No proposition or task is attempted without consideration. Because such people are dependable their superiors trust and help them. Saturn steadies the character, gives them the power to concentrate and makes them philosophical. With such aspects the native is fitted for responsibility and often ends at the head of affairs.

Moon in Conjunction with Saturn: ☽ ☌ ♄

Though the depressing influence of Saturn so close to the emotional centre leads to bouts of despair and makes the subject a doleful character, it is not a bad aspect. He will go through life with a sober outlook.

Moon Square Saturn; Moon Opposition Saturn: ☽ □ ♄; ☽ ☍ ♄

Saturn weighs heavily, making the native a dull, pessimistic character, one who sees traps and snares everywhere and suspects even his best friends. He is unbending and bitter and, though Saturn provides the determination to get on, his schemes come to naught. Should Mars also be badly aspected he is likely to be tricky and not above 'putting over a fast one'. He blames everyone for lack of success and unpopularity.

Moon Trine Uranus; Moon Sextile Uranus: ☽ △ ♅; ☽ ⚹ ♅

Feelings and emotions are affected in unusual ways which make for eccentricity and a desire for new contacts all the time. Women with such aspects are inclined to be flirtatious but with all the natives the imagination is stimulated and there is a hankering after the unusual, and an interest in the occult. If scientifically inclined there should be an inventive faculty for the newer sciences: radio, TV, interplanetary travel, atomic power, etc.

Moon in Conjunction with Uranus: ☽ ☌ ♅

Generally regarded as favourable, but if Venus is badly placed the native might be erotic.

Moon Square Uranus; Moon Opposition Uranus: ☽ □ ♅; ☽ ☍ ♅

As both moon and Uranus make for change this points to frequent changes in residence and a gipsy-like way of living. Artists, hippies and others none too fond of nine-to-five jobs or a hard grind, are thus afflicted. The unusual and the exciting draws such people, who vacillate between enthusiasm and revulsion. They have a false sense of dignity and are apt to think too much of themselves.

Moon Trine Neptune; Moon Sextile Neptune:
  ☽ △ ♆ ; ☽ ⚹ ♆

Both are emotional signs and when well aspected endow the native with a talent for music and acting. They give imagination, love of beauty, sensitivity, an intuitive feeling, and a love for travel abroad.

Moon in Conjunction with Neptune: ☽ ☌ ♆

The influences of moon and Neptune blend admirably to endow the native with psychic insight and in all probability make him a prophetic dreamer or a seer of visions.

Moon Square Neptune; Moon Opposition Neptune:
  ☽ □ ♆ ; ☽ ☍ ♆

The changeability of the moon and the unreliability of Neptune between them produce a type who finds it hard to distinguish fact from fiction and lives in a world of fantasy. If Mercury is badly aspected as well he will need a strong character to prevent him from being dishonest. A tendency to dabble in Black Magic and kindred arts.

Mercury Conjunct Venus; Mercury Sextile Venus:
  ☿ ☌ ♀ ; ☿ ⚹ ♀

Mercury and Venus are never in trine as the widest angle between them is 76 degrees.

Optimistic and ebullient, with a feeling for beauty, harmony, art and literature. Pleasant, amusing, with a love of social life and the ability to learn easily. Profession will depend on the positions of other planets: if Mercury is strong there will be a leaning towards literature, publicity, lecturing, travel or even commerce; if Venus is well placed, the theatre, cinema, radio, TV or the arts will attract the native.

Mercury Trine Mars; Mercury Sextile Mars: ☿ △ ♂;
☿ ✳ ♂

Mars provides energy; Mercury intellect and wit. The native will be good at discussion and arrive at logical conclusions easily, and there will be much enthusiasm, and manual dexterity. A fine analytical brain which can be used in business, detection or diagnosis. Success comes by pushing one's own ideas.

Mercury in Conjunction with Mars: ☿ ♂ ♂
Energy and impulsiveness are too closely concentrated so that everything is larger than life. If this tendency can be curbed, all will be well. A favourable aspect unless either planet is weak or badly placed.

Mercury Square Mars; Mercury Opposition Mars:
☿ ☐ ♂; ☿ ☍ ♂
Here energy and quickness of mind are badly blended to produce a person who is sarcastic instead of witty; quarrelsome instead of reasonable. Action without due thought brings business troubles, overwork and stress. In all, an unstable character.

Mercury Trine Jupiter; Mercury Sextile Jupiter; Mercury in Conjunction with Jupiter: ☿ △ ♃;
☿ ✳ ♃; ☿ ♂ ♃
All three make for a harmonious interaction of the planets to produce a law-abiding, tolerant, thinking person who sees problems clearly and tackles them logically. Generous, open, and a sound judge. As such people decide only on facts and not emotions they make excellent scientists and official referees.

Mercury Square Jupiter; Mercury Opposition Jupiter: ☿ ☐ ♃; ☿ ☍ ♃
The intellect is badly affected and judgement unsound

so that trouble will possibly ensue through errors in contracts and legal matters. There is a tendency to set down in writing remarks that may lead to serious consequences, legally and otherwise.

Mercury Trine Saturn; Mercury Sextile Saturn: ☿ △ ♄; ☿ ✶ ♄

Mercury makes for a clear, incisive intellect; Saturn for profundity and deliberation, and the combination makes slow but sound thinkers. Here we have a steady, orthodox native of great determination and perspicacity; one whom you can trust in all things; utterly reliable.

Mercury in Conjunction with Saturn: ☿ ☌ ♄

The juxtaposition of these planets makes for pessimism, introspection and timidity.

Mercury Square Saturn; Mercury Opposition Saturn: ☿ □ ♄; ☿ ☍ ♄

Here heavy Saturn has a dampening effect on the mind which makes the native magnify his problems. He misses chances because he can't make up his mind and this makes him bitter and fearful. He keeps very much to himself and is inclined to be pernickety. If the chart is otherwise well aspected he will develop into a serious thinker.

Mercury Trine Uranus; Mercury Sextile Uranus: ☿ △ ♅; ☿ ✶ ♅

Mercury makes for a keen intellect; Uranus a love for the unusual, a combination that produces an inventive mind: fiction writer, inventor, investigator, researcher; one who is constantly making new and interesting contacts. Good astrologers have this sign.

Mercury Square Uranus; Mercury Opposition Uranus: ☿ □ ♅; ☿ ☍ ♅

Tends to create the 'kinky' character; the seeker after the novel and the sensational; the exhibitionist and the eccentric. An unstable character.

Mercury Trine Neptune; Mercury Sextile Neptune: ☿ △ ♆; ☿ ⚹ ♆

A combination of mind and imagination that makes for eloquence and the ability to clothe words beautifully, as poets do. The native will be entertaining but also aesthetic; and if Mercury and Neptune be well aspected, he will be psychic.

Mercury Square Neptune; Mercury Opposition Neptune: ☿ □ ♆; ☿ ☍ ♆

The high thinking of Mercury will be muddled by the too-fervid imagination of Neptune, which leads to lack of clear thought and even dishonesty. Such people can't concentrate or manage their affairs and take to prevarication and day dreaming.

Venus Trine Mars; Venus Sextile Mars: ♀ △ ♂; ♀ ⚹ ♂

The native is ardently affectionate and socially ambitious. He will be popular and friends will help him. Very charming with a love of the more showy sports at which he can cut a dash. Good in business, but generous.

Venus in Conjunction with Mars: ♀ ☌ ♂

A strongly sensual nature. No half measures; often acts without due thought. The native usually likes or dislikes at first sight. Too impulsive.

Venus Square Mars; Venus Opposition Mars: ♀ □ ♂;
♀ ☍ ♂

Excessive love of pleasure and uncontrolled passions;
inordinate jealousy causes most of his love affairs to end
unhappily. Coarse, violent nature. Partnerships and
marriage bring financial loss.

Venus Trine Jupiter; Venus Sextile Jupiter: ♀ △ ♃;
♀ ✶ ♃

Fair minded, well balanced, open type who gravitates
to company of his own kind. Venus gives impeccable
taste for decoration, so he likes the best, which is more
often than not the most costly. Well mannered, kind and
without the slightest semblance of jealousy.

Venus Square Jupiter; Venus Opposition Jupiter:
♀ □ ♃; ♀ ☍ ♃

Unfair to those he loves. The sort who stands drinks all
round though he cannot afford it; buys popularity.
Careless, extravagant, lacking in judgement where
speculation is concerned. Has love affairs though
married.

Venus Trine Saturn; Venus Sextile Saturn: ♀ △ ♄;
♀ ✶ ♄

Slow to show affection, which is deep and unchanging.
Slow, too, to marry; sets his sights and reaches the target
regardless of time. Sound and practical in business;
economically wise, simple tastes, honest. Will probably
live a long, serene life.

Venus in Conjunction with Saturn: ♀ ☌ ♄

Once in love, always in love, in an undemonstrative,
even sad fashion. A good friend rather than an ardent
lover. His word is his bond, unless Saturn is badly
aspected elsewhere; and a good payer.

Venus Square Saturn; Venus Opposition Saturn:
    ♀ □ ♄; ♀ ☍ ♄

Love life frequently goes awry causing depression and disillusion. Elders disapprove of his choice, engagements tend to be drawn out; there may be wide differences in the ages of one partner and the other; and his wife may be forever ailing. Indecisive in business, clinching deals at the wrong times. A general air of hopelessness.

Venus Trine Uranus; Venus Sextile Uranus: ♀ △ ♅;
    ♀ ⚹ ♅

Artistically original and unconventional. A strong personality. Tendency to fall in love at first sight and has a magnetic effect on the opposite sex. Unusual likes and dislikes and unusual experiences in love. Friendships and gains made suddenly and unexpectedly.

Venus Square Uranus; Venus Opposition Uranus:
    ♀ □ ♅; ♀ ☍ ♅

The makings of a libertine. Marries quickly, without due thought, and is divorced or separated perhaps many times, depending on other aspects. Has exaggerated ideas about independence and personal freedom.

Venus Trine Neptune; Venus Sextile Neptune; Venus in Conjunction with Neptune: ♀ △ ♆;
    ♀ ⚹ ♆; ♀ ☌ ♆

These favourable combinations produce musical and artistic talent, and friendships with artistic people who make life worth living. An intriguing personality which greatly attracts the opposite sex.

Venus Square Neptune; Venus Opposition Neptune:
    ♀ □ ♆; ♀ ☍ ♆

Passions for unscrupulous partners; faithlessness in matrimony; deception in love. He will let his partner down, break his word, cause scandal and attract unfortunate publicity. Bad judge of character who makes friends with unreliable people.

Mars Trine Jupiter; Mars Sextile Jupiter: ♂ △ ♃; ♂ ✶ ♃

Mars gives strength and energy, Jupiter a love of justice and fair play; the combined influences produce an open type who will fight to the death against injustice and wrong. The native will respect the law and keep his word irrespective of documents and bonds. Good leaders whether in business, the professions or the armed forces, who have a strong sense of duty and executive ability.

Mars in Conjunction with Jupiter: ♂ ☌ ♃

The nearness of these planets may lead to explosions and a tendency to take the law into one's own hands, especially if they are badly placed. Other aspects must be considered, however, before reaching a conclusion. Also an indication of wealth.

Mars Square Jupiter; Mars Opposition Jupiter: ♂ □ ♃; ♂ ☍ ♃

Here judgement is clouded by personal likes and dislikes and if a bad cause is embraced it will be defended tooth and nail. The sense of justice is upset. A boaster who spends too heavily, falls into difficulties through inattention to financial matters; impulsive; hot tempered.

Mars Trine Saturn; Mars Sextile Saturn: ♂ △ ♄; ♂ ✶ ♄

Saturn's tenacity combines favourably with the energy and strength of Mars. Once the native gets his teeth into a problem he sees it through. Brave, confident, untiring; a type that makes good soldiers, engineers, miners and even lawyers. Practical, materialistic, down-to-earth;

a trifle ruthless; perhaps cold. But in all, good and honest.

Mars in Conjunction with Saturn: ♂ ♂ ♄
Generally speaking, favourable; but Saturn slows all enterprises, which are held back, making the native depressed, selfish and apt to be somewhat cruel. Here again, other aspects must be noted.

Mars Square Saturn; Mars Opposition Saturn:
   ♂ ☐ ♄; ♂ ☍ ♄
Hard, cruel, self-seeking, without a care for others. They neither trust nor are trusted and their whole attitude towards life makes enemies. They have few saving graces and repel.

Mars Trine Uranus; Mars Sextile Uranus: ♂ △ ♅;
   ♂ ✳ ♅
The inventive side of the native is given full scope by his energy and initiative. Constructive and inventive in industrial and research work. A very positive type.

Mars in Conjunction with Uranus: ♂ ♂ ♅
An unusual type; eccentric to extremes; energetic and inventive but not thorough. Often decides problems without due thought or examination.

Mars Square Uranus; Mars Opposition Uranus:
   ♂ ☐ ♅; ♂ ☍ ♅
Forceful but unconstructive. No real direction; often vacillates but can be as stubborn as a camel. Unpredictable. Criminals, adventurers and anarchists have these aspects, but in combination with good aspects these men make daring and unorthodox military commanders.

Mars Trine Neptune; Mars Sextile Neptune: ♂ △ ♆ ;
♂ ⚹ ♆

Mars provides enthusiasm and energy; Neptune a liking
for the occult and mystic. The native gravitates towards
surgery and if Neptune aspects are powerful, the sea.
Apt to dabble in drugs.

Mars Square Neptune; Mars Opposition Neptune:
♂ □ ♆ ; ♂ ☍ ♆

The energy of Mars takes a destructive form and makes
the native vindictive, 'kinky', unable to settle and concentrate or stay in one place for long. He is attracted
to the wrong types, or may lead others astray, depending
on other aspects.

Jupiter Trine Saturn; Jupiter Sextile Saturn: ♃ △ ♄ ;
♃ ⚹ ♄

A serious, stable, honest type; utterly trustworthy.
Inclined to science or philosophy and a sound judge in
all matters. Though Saturn tends to delay success, this
comes, in all probability, during the second half of life.

Jupiter in Conjunction with Saturn: ♃ ☌ ♄

A good, reliable subject, thorough and deliberate in all
he does, though there will be an absence of warmth and
humour in the nature.

Jupiter Square Saturn; Jupiter Opposition Saturn:
♃ □ ♄ ; ♃ ☍ ♄

Jupiter's fairness and sound judgement will be nullified
by Saturn which will make the native suspicious, 'cagey'
and unsympathetic. If the head of a family he will be
a 'Barrett of Wimpole Street'. Tendency to resort to the
law which may be catastrophic. Disliked by all.

Jupiter Trine Uranus; Jupiter Sextile Uranus:
♃ △ ♅; ♃ ⚹ ♅

Jupiter represents wisdom and Uranus inventiveness and the combination makes for unusual, out-of-the-way philosophies, inventiveness and novel schemes. The native is original and takes a wide view of life. Interested in the humanities and science with a special bent for research.

Jupiter Square Uranus; Jupiter Opposition Uranus:
♃ □ ♅; ♃ ☍ ♅

Clouded judgement which leads to impracticable schemes resulting in financial loss. Errors of judgement in speculation and research, to which the native is drawn; and he is likely to fall foul of authority.

Jupiter Trine Neptune; Jupiter Sextile Neptune:
♃ △ ♆; ♃ ⚹ ♆

As Jupiter gives sound judgement and Neptune a mystical quality there will be a love of beauty, ultra-modern music and the occult. Sound intuition will make speculation successful. Fondness for travel, especially by sea, and an interest in metaphysics.

Jupiter in Conjunction with Neptune: ♃ ☌ ♆
Unless Jupiter is weak or badly aspected, in which case the native will have hunches that go wrong, this is considered a favourable aspect.

Jupiter Square Neptune; Jupiter Opposition Neptune: ♃ □ ♆; ♃ ☍ ♆
Neptunian fantasy overrides the sound judgement of Jupiter, making the native superstitious to a degree and giving him a tendency to dabble in cranky religions. Also, he is often in legal trouble.

Saturn Trine Uranus; Saturn Sextile Uranus: ♄ △ ♅; ♄ ⚹ ♅

Determination and the ability to concentrate on practical matters gives the native an inventive turn and makes him competent in any branch of engineering.

Saturn in Conjunction with Uranus: ♄ ☌ ♅

Generally a good aspect, though there is tendency to suffer ill health. Pay strict attention to diet.

Saturn Square Uranus; Saturn Opposition Uranus: ♄ □ ♅; ♄ ☍ ♅

Inventiveness borders on fantasy and ideas and schemes come to naught. They are impracticable but are persisted in through egotism and this results in vile temper.

Saturn Trine Neptune; Saturn Sextile Neptune: ♄ △ ♆; ♄ ⚹ ♆

Sound, deep thinker possessing a strong psychic tendency which will prove invaluable in investment and speculation. Interested in oil, chemistry and shipping.

Saturn in Conjunction with Neptune; Saturn Square Neptune; Saturn Opposition Neptune: ♄ ☌ ♆; ♄ □ ♆; ♄ ☍ ♆

Dangerous experiments in psychic matters unbalance the mind. Liable to indulge in crazy investments and be cheated by friends and those one trusts.

Uranus Trine Neptune; Uranus Sextile Neptune: ♅ △ ♆; ♅ ⚹ ♆

Astrologers and all keenly interested in the occult have these aspects in their charts. So do those who are attracted by metaphysics, or who indulge in bizarre experiments and secret activities, such as spies. Anything secret or unusual appeals to such people.

Uranus in Conjunction with Neptune; Uranus Square Neptune; Uranus Opposition Neptune:
♅ ☌ ♆; ♅ □ ♆; ♅ ☍ ♆

The native is likely to have an adventurous, unsettled life, alternating between success and failure. Extremely individualistic and subject to moods and presentiments. Occult experiments may bring trouble.

Parts of the Astrological Jig-Saw

Aspects are but parts of the astrological jig-saw. Interpretations must be made not by aspects alone, but by their relation to other aspects, planets and signs and the houses in which they fall. There are entire books devoted to the study of the aspects, the best probably for the beginner being *The Principles of Astrology* by the late C. O. E. Carter, dean of British astrologers in his time, who dealt with the subject comprehensively and in a way that all can understand. Study that and you will realize that it is pointless to try to interpret a horoscope until the fundamentals, such as the aspects, have been mastered.

CHAPTER SIX

HEALTH FROM THE HOROSCOPE

In the distant past the leading physicians used astrology to understand their patients and diagnose their ailments because they realized that the signs influenced the body, depending on their positions in the chart and the aspects of the planets.

Men like Dee, Lilley, Culpeper, Gerard and others combined medicine and astrology effectively. During the eighteenth century (the Age of Reason) which saw the rise of the materialistic school of philosophy (D'Alembert, Bayle, Buffon, Condillac, Condorcet, Diderot, D'Holbach, La Mettrie, Montesquieu, Rousseau and Voltaire) astrology fell into disrepute, mountebanks and charlatans abounded and the art was discredited.

Today, however, there is an increasing body of medical men, osteopaths, chiropractors and herbalists who combine astrology with the healing arts with astonishing success.

Aries
Aries rules the head and brain, eyes, face, upper jaw and the carotid arteries. Thumb back the pages to a description of the signs and you will see that the Aries is a man of action for the sign is ruled by Mars, a planet that is fiery and arid, inflammatory, eruptive, and violent. It rules sport, athletics and war, so naturally the Aries native is quick-tempered and explosive.

Aries generates heat, so when the native is down with colds, influenza and other illnesses in which the temperature rises above 98.4° Fah., that of the Aries patient will be two or three degrees higher than in patients born under watery signs, under similar conditions.

Typical Aries diseases are neuralgia, brain fever, congestion of the brain, baldness, headache, dizziness, eye diseases, toothache, gumboils.

Aries natives are strong willed, however, and when seriously ill make a fight to regain health, which always assists the healing process. They love life and hate to relinquish their hold on it and as they help the physician in every possible way, make excellent patients.

Taurus
Diseases are, of course, typical of the signs under which patients are born. Taurus is a stolid, bull-necked fellow

and the sign rules neck, ears, palate, larynx, tonsils, the thyroid gland, lower jaw, the cerebellum, the back of the head, the atlas and cervical vertebrae, carotid arteries, jugular vein and pharynx.

Taurus is ruled by Venus which influences the throat, kidneys, thymus gland and the venous circulation.

The Taurean is noted for his stubborness. He will neither give way nor let go. He does the same with diseases. When he contracts one he clings to it tenaciously. He fears illness and because of this the typical Taurean rarely makes a good patient, or a good doctor or nurse. Unlike the Aries native who has little fear of disease and tries to get rid of it as soon as possible, the Taurean has a tendency to be a hypochondriac and often falls a victim to disease because he fears it.

Being stocky the native nearly always puts on flesh after thirty and later develops a double chin and a fat neck. The most common Taurean diseases are goitre, diphtheria, laryngitis, tonsillitis, croup, polypus, quinsy, glandular swelling of the throat, and apoplexy, which is not surprising when one knows that the ruler of Taurus is Venus which influences throat, the thymus gland, kidneys and the venous circulation.

Gemini
Gemini influences the arms, hands, shoulders, lungs, thymus gland, upper ribs, trachea, bronchi, the very tiny veins near the surface and at the extremities of hands and feet, breath and blood.

Mercury rules Gemini and among other things has a powerful effect on the nerves, the pulmonary circulation, vocal chords, eyes, ears and tongue, and the senses.

The natives are quick and nervy and are afflicted more than any other type by neuresthenia. Unlike Taureans,

Geminians take little interest in health or the habits that conserve it. They catch colds easily and tuberculosis takes a heavier toll among them than natives in any other of the signs. They are not sickly, however, for their mental approach helps them to throw off illness easily; but they are prone to diseases of the lungs, such as bronchitis; asthma and pleurisy, and of course, nervous diseases.

Cancer

Cancer is ruled by the moon whose rays influence the oesophagus, uterus, ovaries, lymphatic and sympathetic nervous systems, synovial fluid, alimentary canal and the nerve sheaths. Consequently the native is prone to suffer from troubles of the stomach, diaphragm, liver, thoracic duct, digestion, pancreas and serum of the blood. Many under this sign have stomach ulcers and women suffer from mammae troubles.

They love their food and have a tendency to overeat and this leads to digestive trouble, protracted hiccoughing, flatulency and, as Cancer is a water sign, dropsy. Their diseases are those caused by faulty diet, especially if Saturn happens to be in Cancer for we know that Saturn has a cramping, crabbing, retrogressive influence, and there will be an over-fondness for pastries, pies and sweets.

If Cancer is rising in the chart then vitality will be low, sound advice about diet will be ignored, for this makes the native hypersensitive and suspicious and he will do the exact opposite.

But if by judicious praise or appreciation the confidence of the native can be won, he will co-operate willingly. If the sun, source of life and energy, is in Cancer, the native's vitality will be vastly increased. This will be apparent by their own positions and the positions of the planets in relation to them.

Leo
Leo is ruled by the sun and if the sign is on the Ascendant the native will be charged with much energy and a sound constitution, almost impervious to illness. He does not succumb easily and when ill recovers with astonishing speed. He is a proud being to whom illness is tantamount to physical defeat; and this sometimes proves his undoing.

He puts far more energy into activities than is necessary; often more than his body can endure and as a result typical Leo diseases are those of the heart, angina pectoris, the spinal cord — especially the dorsal region.

The spine is the centre of energy and the seat of bodily strength and the vital spinal fluid is influenced and regulated by Leo and those born with Leo rising prove exceptionally tough; but if destructive aspects are at work this energy is channelled along the wrong lines and the native will be afflicted by heart and spinal troubles, and disturbances of the spleen will have a direct effect, also white corpuscles will multiply in the blood. This will bring about anaemia — sometimes pernicious anaemia — which until recently has invariably resulted in death. So the very gifts of Leo may cause destruction if unwisely used.

Virgo
Virgo, second of the Earth signs, is negative and feminine and endows the body with lesser powers of resistance, for instance, than Leo. Like Geminians, the natives of Virgo are ruled by Mercury and are wiry and fretful in temperament. When they go under they have difficulty in fighting their way back to health; they are pawns of events and circumstances rather than dictators of them.

Virgo is, of course, the natural Sixth House sign, the house that rules over sickness, so it is unfortunate when Virgoans get the idea into their heads that they are very ill because if so they tend to degenerate into chronic invalids. The medical cupboard of a typical native resembles a chemist's shop.

Because of their empathy with the sick, those born under Virgo make understanding and sympathetic nurses and sick rooms are filled with them. Unfortunately, many of them are liable to take on the afflictions and complaints of those to whom they administer.

Their bowels are their weakest organ and constipation is a typical Virgoan disease. They also suffer from diarrhoea, appendicitis, peritonitis (both the outcome of constipation), cholera (if living in the tropics), dysentry, worms and catarrh of the bowels. Stomach cramp and wind are among their minor afflictions, for Virgo rules stomach, intestines, liver, spleen, duodenum and the sympathetic nervous system which controls this region.

Libra

Though both Taurus and Libra are ruled by Venus, the native Libran is not noted for ruggedness of constitution because the sun is weak in this sign. As it enters the sign it changes from north to south and its rays are less powerful than at other periods of the year.

Librans are perhaps the most sensitive of all the signs with moods that vary between exhilaration and despondency. They are the world's idealists and if their idols are shown to have feet of clay they can be plunged into despair which may result in illness, for as we know now, more than half our ailments are emotional or caused by undue stress.

Libra rules the kidneys, the lumbar region, skin, ureters and the vaso-motor system which affects the walls of the blood vessels. The diseases, therefore, that the native is most likely to suffer from are Bright's disease, which is a breakdown of kidney function, lumbago, and urinary trouble, the result of malfunctioning kidneys.

Much of course, depends on the position of the planets. If afflicted by Saturn, micturition is difficult; if by Jupiter there will be excessive urination. Nephritis and diabetes are common Libran diseases so care must be paid to diet; carbohydrates and sugars should be cut down and more fresh fruit and salads consumed. The native is also likely to be pestered by eczema and kindred skin troubles.

Scorpio

As Scorpio is ruled by Mars, which is fiery and explosive, the native is generally assumed to be an unpleasant, bad tempered, cruel type, eager to enter into acrimonious argument, who will push his opinions to the bitter end. Fortunately for those born under this sign, there are many types of Scorpion; some secretive and retiring to the point of becoming recluses.

The native is often sensual, with strong emotions which are often his own undoing.

Scorpio rules the bladder, prostate gland, pubic bone, bones of the nose and haemoglobin, and his afflictions are usually those of the organs of generation and the ducts and passages through which excretions pass.

Though the native may appear to be unfeeling and dictatorial, Scorpios make the best healers — doctors and surgeons — for the healer must be something of a dictator whose rulings have to be accepted.

The bad type allows the sensual side of his nature to dominate, indulges in excesses and if the planets are afflicting, may suffer from syphilis, hernia, scurvy, fistula, piles, nasal catarrh and, in women, inflammation of the womb and fallen womb, and uterine troubles.

Stricture of the prostate gland is a common Scorpio affliction, the cause of which has not yet been determined.

Sagittarius

Sagittarius is ruled by kindly Jupiter and being frank and trusting puts his faith in his medical adviser and is soon halfway on the road to recovery. He is, however, more open to suggestion than any other sign and thoughts and fears implanted in his mind that he is seriously ill and getting worse, retard his recovery.

Being an open-air type he is usually active, healthy and robust.

The loins, hips, sacral region, coccygeal vertebrae, femus, ilium, arteries of the iliac, and sciatic nerves are ruled by Sagittarius.

Typical Sagittarian diseases are sciatica and rheumatism, hip-joint disease, and locomotor ataxia, a chronic nervous disease which is also one of the results of tertial syphilis and ten times as common in men as in women. In this terrible affliction the conducting paths from the spinal cord which carry messages from the nerves in the limbs, to the brain, are destroyed, with a complete inability to co-ordinate movements. Thus, for instance, if a victim closes his eyes and wants to touch the tip of his nose, his fingers don't know where to go and he succeeds only when he can see.

Capricorn

Capricornians are the toughest of the human race. The sign, as we know, is an Earth one and ruled by Saturn. A typical native is Saturnine in appearance, wiry and solemn. He has to be really ill before he will take to his bed.

Saturn makes her subjects extremely tenacious and once a disease implants itself in the system it is not easily thrown off and many degenerate into hypochondriacs. Tact and suggestion are needed to counteract the conviction that they are seriously ill.

Unfortunately they do not accept advice willingly

when ill and as they are sensitive and retiring, retreat into their shells like tortoises. Never at the best of times gay and sparkling they become pessimistic under the dark pall of disease and often automatically deteriorate. Once in the cold clamp of illness they take long to recover.

Capricorn rules the knees, skin, joints and hair; that is why the typical native has a dry, sallow skin and lank mousy hair.

The diseases to which they are prone more than other natives are eczema, syphilis, and leprosy; this last only if they live in the tropics. They are ungraceful and do not move easily; dislocation of bones is a common complaint with them.

Aquarius

Aquarius as we know, is a fixed Air sign with dual rulers: the sad inhibiting Saturn which obstructs at every turn, and the impulsive, emotional, even hysterical Uranus. Being born under a fixed sign the Aquarian has an inflexible will; but if Saturn and Uranus are strongly aspected he will be moved to extremes of moods, falling into black troughs of despondency, or rising to peaks of emotional ecstasy under the influence of Uranus. Such alternating moods inevitably take their toll of the nervous system, with resulting ill health.

Aquarians are apt to live on their nerves and push their bodies beyond sensible limits. Then they crack up and have nervous breakdowns but unlike Capricornians they heed advice and help in the curative process.

Diseases typical of their sign are the nervous diseases; general neuresthenia in particular, varicose veins and swellings of the legs, due usually to obstructed circulation. The Aquarian instinctively knows when his nerves are badly frayed and when to let up for he feels as if tiny insects are crawling all over him, sometimes even under his skin. If he heeds the red light, all will be well.

Pisces

Pisces is a water sign and the typical native has a negative nature which makes him give in too easily or take the line of least resistance, especially where the flesh-pots are concerned. Consequently after thirty or forty he puts on unhealthy, flabby flesh.

He is extremely susceptible to suggestion and when ill, to the ministrations of his doctor. Because of this he should beware the well-meaning sympathizer who leads him to believe that his condition is more dire than it really is. Only the cheerful should be allowed to visit him when ill.

Because of the Neptunian influence Pisceans have a tendency to indulge more in alcohol than they should and often drift into the habit of taking drugs.

Pisces rules the feet, toes and fibrin or clotting mechanism of the blood, and typical diseases are bunions, gout, deformed feet and toes, tumours and dropsy. The true Piscean walks with his feet splayed, like the flippers of a seal.

Interpretation

Not all who are born under a sign are typical natives. Much depends upon the Ascendant, whose ruler has a strong effect upon the native, and the positions of a number of planets in one or more houses may make a tremendous difference, but of course, he will inherently be strongly influenced by the sign under which he was born.

This is what makes astrology such an absorbing study and why some horoscopes are infinitely more difficult to unravel than others. If the whole thing were cut and dried anyone would become an expert; whereas, though it is possible for everyone to draw up and read a chart, it needs study, hard work and an inborn flair to do so expertly.

CHAPTER SEVEN

SETTING UP A NATAL CHART

Before setting up a Horoscope or Natal Chart you should
know the exact time, date and place in which the subject
was born. Armed with these facts no other information
is needed, but though almost every one knows the date
of his or her birth, few know the exact time. In Scotland
and in some other countries the time is given on the birth
certificate, but not in England, Wales or Ireland. In
India, where everyone who can afford it has his horoscope
drawn up, the time of birth is meticulously noted so that
the baby's progress throughout life can be charted.

The Suspicious Client
In Britain, when a subject is asked the time of birth, the
query is passed on to the mother, who says: 'You came
in time for tea,' or 'I know it was about noon because
it was a Saturday and your father came straight from
work to the hospital.' On such vague directions the
astrologer is supposed to draw up an accurate chart,
though as little as twenty minutes can make a significant
difference. So, in order to arrive at the exact time the
astrologer asks his clients a number of questions, which
makes them suspicious.

'Ah,' they say, 'you want me to tell you! But that's
what I'm paying you for.'

The Purpose of Questions
Questions or a personal visit are of value *only* when the
exact time of birth is not known. From height, build, face,
colouring and movements the type can be placed with
certainty; and important events in life, such as the death

of parents, marriage, etc., will help to rectify errors. The astrologer acts in much the same way as a doctor who diagnoses by the colour of the tongue and eyes, skin, state of breath, pulse, heartbeat, blood pressure, urine, symptoms you describe and your medical history. Yet, patients are never suspicious of a doctor's questions, or suspect his motives.

Like medicine, astrology is not magic. The more you learn about it and the more horoscopes you interpret, the more skilled you will become, till eventually a quick glance at a chart will reveal much about a client.

The Ephemeris

To erect a chart you need an *Ephemeris* (Greek: *ephemera*, a day), which gives the positions of the planets on every day of the year. Unfortunately, an Ephemeris cannot be consulted in a public library as it is not considered essential literature. It is issued annually and you can buy one for the year you want, or buy them in bound volumes for sixty years at a stretch.

Raphael's Ephemeris gives the positions of the Sun, Moon and planets for every day of the year, calculated for noon at Greenwich Mean Time, or GMT.

The Chart

You can buy printed blank charts in packets of twenty-five or fifty but the beginner would be advised to make his own, using compass and ruler, with the illustration of page 80 as an example. It will be seen that the chart is divided into 12 equal parts, each for one of the 12 houses.

The Erection of a Horoscope

Let us assume that the subject is a girl born in London as 12 a.m. (noon) on 30 September 1968. Open your Ephemeris at page 18 and run your pencil down the

Date of Birth: 30.9.1968 (London), 9 a.m. BST = 8 a.m. GMT
Placidus Cusps

THE HOROSCOPE

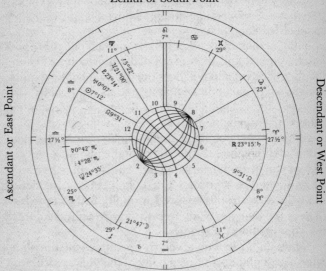

Zenith or South Point

Ascendant or East Point

Descendant or West Point

Nadir or North Point

PLANET	LAT.	DECL.	ASPECTS									
			☉	☽	☿	♀	♂	♃	♄	♅	♆	♇
Sun........☉		2°56′S					⊼			♂	L	
Moon .....☽		26°40′S					⊒	△	□		✳	△
Mercury...☿		15°04′S				♂	✳					
Venus......♀		13°00′S			P		✳	L				L
Mars........♂		10°41′N										
Jupiter ....♃		4°31′N							⊼		✳	♂
Saturn .....♄		6°27′N							P			⊼
Uranus ...♅		0°36′N										
Neptune..♆		17°18′S										✳
Pluto ......♇		16°20′N									P	

extreme left hand column. This gives the days of the month. The adjacent column shows that she was born on a Monday, which is of no significance as far as her horoscope is concerned.

The next column is headed Sidereal Time or Star Time, which reads 12 hours 37 minutes and 11 seconds. All positions in the Ephemeris are calculated at Noon.

Tables of Houses
Now turn to the Tables of Houses for London, on the pages after 41, and glance down the column marked Sidereal Time. Look for the time closest to 12h 37m 11s. It is 12h 37m 45s, a difference of 26 seconds, which you can ignore. It will have no effect on the horoscope.

The Tenth House
The next column is <u>10</u> which means that the Tenth House is in Libra. The number on the right of 12h 36m 45s is 10, which means that the Tenth House starts on the Tenth degree of Libra.

Now we can begin to fill in the chart. Place <u>10</u> over the vertical line at the top of the chart, known as the Cusp, which forms the beginning of the Tenth House and is known as the Mid-Heaven of the native's horoscope.

Eleventh House
The next column, going counter-clockwise, is headed <u>11</u> but on the fourth line down you will see the sign ♏ (Scorpio), which means that the Eleventh House is in that sign. Run your pencil down the column till it is opposite 12h 36m 45s and the number will be 6, so mark it in the chart as ♏ 6.

Twelfth House
Move to the next column on the right, which is also headed by Scorpio. Run your pencil down till it is

opposite 12h 36m 45s and the number will be 25, so fill
it in as Scorpio 25 or ♏ 25.

Ascendant of First House, or Ascen

The next column is headed Ascen Sagittarius; you will
notice that the sign has changed. Run your pencil down
till it is opposite 12h 36m 45s and the numbers will be
10 degrees 15 minutes ♐ . Fill them in at the top of the
horizontal line on the left hand side of your chart: ♐
10° 15'.

Second House

You will notice in the next column that the sign has gone
into Capricorn ♑ and opposite 12h 36m 45s the number
is 18. So fill it in as ♑ 18.

Third House

Under 3 you will see that the sign has changed to ♒
(Aquarius), but seven lines down it changes once again
to Pisces ♓ and opposite 12h 36m 45s is the number
3, so fill it in as ♓ 3.

The signs for six houses have now been filled in; but
there are twelve. Each house has an opposite house:

> Aries   is opposite Libra
> Taurus is opposite Scorpio
> Gemini is opposite Sagittarius
> Cancer is opposite Capricorn
> Leo   is opposite Aquarius
> Virgo   is opposite Pisces

These lie opposite in the chart and always bear the
same degree. So fill them in.

The Missing Sun
There are, as you know, 12 signs and all must appear
in the chart. But if you look at the chart you have just
filled in you will find that Aquarius ♒ is missing; so add
it in the order in which it normally appears; that is, after
Capricorn ♑. And, as the sign opposite Aquarius is
always Leo, fill this in exactly opposite 18 ♌. These are
known as 'intercepted signs'.

The Sun ☉
Turn back to page 18 and run your pencil down the
column headed Long. with the sign of the Sun above
it till it is opposite 30 September. The reading will be
7° 22′ 57″ and eight lines above you will see the sign
Libra.
   Now Libra ♎ is on the Cusp of the chart: and as 7°
22′ 57″ is less than 10, write the sign of the Sun and 7°
22′ 57″ to the right of the vertical line. Had it been greater
than 10 it would be to the left.

The Moon ☽
Run down the column marked Moon Long. and
opposite the 30th you will see 24° 7′ 49″ in the sign of
Sagittarius. A glance at your chart will show that
Sagittarius is in the Second House and as 24 is more than
18 put the sign of the Moon and 24° 7′ 49″ on the left
hand sign of the line.
   Now we come to the planets, which you will find on
page 44.

Neptune ♆
The second column is headed Neptune Long. and on
the first line is the sign Scorpio ♏; so write down the
longitude and the sign, in the chart: 24° 35′.

Uranus ♅

Uranus is next. You will see that on the first of the month Uranus is in ♍ but on the 28th it changes to and on the 30th it is in 0° 7' in ♎: so fill that in.

Saturn ♄

On the first of the month Saturn, the third planet is in 23° 15' Aries. On the 2nd it starts to Retrograde; that is, move backwards through the sign, so we see an **R** to indicate this. On the 30th it is 23° 15' in Aries: 23° 15' **R** ♈.

Jupiter ♃

Jupiter is next and we see that the planet has moved into Virgo: 21° 1'.

Mars ♂

On the 1st Mars is in ♌ but by the 24th it moves into Virgo ♍ and on the 30th is 5° 28' ♏.

Venus ♀

On the 1st Venus is in ♏; on the 2nd it moves into ♎ and on the 28th into ♎ 4° 40'.

Mercury ☿

Mercury which on the 1st lay in ♍, passed into ♎ on the 2nd, but on the 29th moved into ♏ and on the 30th it was 0° 46' ♍.

The Nodes

When you have filled these details into their respective houses there remain only the Nodes of the Moon to be added. Their positions are given in the extreme right hand column on the top half of the page, under Moon Node. The Node here refers to the North Node of the Moon and its position on the 30th is 5☽ 9° 31' ♈. Fill this into the Third House, and exactly opposite, in the Tenth House, fill in the position of the South Node.

Well-Tried Formula

Do not worry your head about the reasons for these various moves. The formula is one that has stood the test of centuries and you must go through the same mechanical process each time you set up a horoscope. Explanations would need another book and even then would be of little practical help. You will find that charts drawn up on these instructions will reflect a true picture of subjects' characters, talents, abilities, likes and dislikes and give a preview of their progress through life.

Clairvoyance and Intuition

An astrologer need not be a clairvoyant or blessed with intuition. Later he will develop a feeling for judging horoscopes just as an experenced physician can diagnose disease in a few seconds without going through all the laborious eliminating processes needed by a student in his final year. What may seem almost impossible today will be easy in six months and second nature in a year. But first, you must learn to walk.

Pars Fortunae (Part of Fortune)

The Part of Fortune gives an indication as to where the subject's luck will lie and is calculated by converting the Ascendant, Moon and Sun into degrees, adding the degrees of the Ascendant and Moon and subtracting the degrees of the Sun. Pencil the answer into the map. It may sound involved but is simple.

In our chart the Ascendant is 10° 15′ Libra or 10¼. As it is less than half we call it 10.

Libra is the 7th sign and as each sign has 30 degrees this makes 210 plus 10 = 220.

The Moon is 18° 46′ Capricorn, which we will call

19, and as Capricorn is the 11th sign: 330 + 19 = 349. So the number of degrees for the Ascendant and Moon = 330 + 220 which adds up to 550.

The Sun is 10° Libra and as Libra is the seventh sign we add 10 + 330 = 340. Now subtract 340 from 550 and the answer is 210. As each sign if 30 degrees, divide 210 by 30 = 7. So the Path of Fortune will lie in Libra.

The Aspects

The chart is now complete but not the horoscope. The Aspects must be set out in such a way that the map can be read at a glance. Before going further let me impress on you that the symbols for the Signs and Planets must be memorized so thoroughly that at the mention of Libra you will instantly see ♎; and when Neptune is mentioned, a trident with a cross below it.

Once you have memorized the symbols and they are photographed in your mind the process of setting up a chart will be comparatively easy.

Then comes the real work of interpreting the chart and reading the horoscope.

CHAPTER EIGHT

ERECTING A HOROSCOPE

Everyone who takes up astrology wants to know how to erect a chart replete with symbols and lines. When this has been mastered the study becomes far more interesting as the character, abilities and limitations of the native* are revealed. Let us assume that he or she was born in London at 9 a.m. B.S.T. (British Summer

*The person whose chart is being drawn up.

Time) which is 8 a.m. G.M.T. (Greenwich Mean Time) on 30 September 1968. Few people, in fact, are born exactly on the hour and in Britain (Scotland excepted) the time of birth is not recorded on the certificate, though in many European countries, and in India and the Far East, it is. If the interval between noon and the time of birth is such as to render the arithmetical division of the movement difficult the positions can be worked out by the use of proportional logarithms, a table of which, with explanation of the method, is given on the last page of the ephemeris. When the astrologer is given no indication of the time of birth the chart may be erected for noon, or for sunrise (with noon positions of the planets) and when this is done it should be indicated above the chart.

Sidereal Time

The length of any day is not 24 hours but 23 hours 56 minutes and 4.09 seconds, which means that the stars rise and set about 3m 56s earlier due to the difference between Solar Time and Sidereal (Latin: *sidus*, star) or Star Time (S.T.). The first step, therefore, is to find the S.T. for birth.

Turn to page 18 of your ephemeris for 1968 and run down the column in the lower half of the page marked Sidereal Time till you reach 30 September. S.T. for noon is 12h 37m 11s. Always work with a short rule as it is easy to look at the wrong line and set down the wrong figures. As the interval between noon and birth is four hours and birth took place *before* noon, subtract four hours. Had it taken place at 4 p.m., four hours would have to be added. So the S.T. at birth is 8h 37m 11s. Seconds can be ignored as they have a negligible effect on the horoscope.

Tables of Houses

Now you can place the signs where they belong in the

chart. The process is a mechanical one and though at first it may appear formidable you can run through it rapidly when the various steps have been mastered. Turn to the unnumbered pages after 41, marked Tables of Houses for London, Latitude 51 32N. Glance down the column headed S.T. and look for the numbers nearest to 8h 37m. You will find them eight lines down in the second column marked S.T.: 8h 37m 37s.

Tenth House
The column on the right is headed 10, which means Tenth House, and under it is the sign ♌. Below is a tiny circle denoting degrees, which means that the numbers in the column relate to the degrees of the sign on the cusp or beginning of the Tenth House. Run your pencil down till it is level with 8h 37m 37s and the number in the column is 7. Pencil this into your chart as 7° ♌.

Eleventh House
The next column on the right bears the sign ♍ and eight lines down is the number 11, which means that the degree on the 11th cusp is 11, so mark that in as 11° ♍.

Twelfth House
In the next column you will see that the sign has changed to ♎ and the degree at the cusp is 8. Mark that in as 8° ♎.

Ascendant or First House (Ascen)
The Ascendant is under the same sign but the cusp is 27° 44' and as 44 is more than half a degree we call it 27½. Pencil it in as 27½ ♎.

Second House
The sign has now changed to ♏ and as the number of degrees is 25, mark it as 25° ♏.

Third House

The sign on the cusp of this house is ♐ and the degrees 29: 29° ♐.

The signs on the cusps of six houses have been filled in; but there are 12 signs, each having an opposite sign bearing the same degree:

> Aries   is opposite Libra
> Taurus is opposite Scorpio
> Gemini is opposite Sagittarius
> Cancer is opposite Capricorn
> Leo   is opposite Aquarius
> Virgo   is opposite Pisces

Missing Signs

Each of the 12 signs must appear in the chart, but in this instance ♑ and ♋ are missing. As ♑ follows ♐ fill it in in that sequence. The sign opposite ♑ is ♋, so fill that in as well, as shown in the chart. In cases such as this, these are known as 'intercepted signs'.

Planetary Positions

The positions of the Sun,* Moon* and Planets must be filled in to complete the chart. As the Moon has considerable movement in 24 hours, this can be found by simple calculation. Turn to page 18 and consult the table in the bottom half of the page.

The Sun

The Sun's longitude on
30 September was: 7° 22′ 57″ ♎
The Sun's longitude on
29 September was: 6° 23′ 58″ ♎

*Though the Sun and Moon are not planets their positions are determined in the same way as those of the planets.

Subtract the second from the
first: 0° 58' 59"
For practical purposes we assume
this to be: 0° 59'

Turn to the Table of Proportional Logarithms on the
last page of the ephemeris. The top left hand column
is headed Min (minutes) and the line running across
Degrees or Hours. The first column indicates minutes
either of mean time or longitude from 0 to 59.

(1) Find the log of the Sun's motion or 0° 59'. by
running down the Min column to 59 and looking under
0. The log is 1.3875.

(2) Find the log of the interval between time of birth
and noon, which is 4 hours. Place your pencil on 4 and
opposite 0 minutes. The log is 7781.

(3) Add 1.3875 to 7781 = 2.1656

(4) Noon position of the Sun is: 7° 22'   ♎

(5) Anti-log (nearest to 2.1656)
is: 0° 10'   ♊

(6) Position at given time is:
7° 22'-0° 10' =   7° 12'   ♎

The Moon
The Moon's position is calculated in the same way. Turn
to page 18 and run down the column marked ☽ long
to 30 September and you will see that the Moon has
travelled from 10° ♑ to 24° ♑ in 24 hours, or a distance
of 13° 58'.

Turn to the page of logs, run along the column to 13
and then down till opposite 58 and the number under
13 is 2351. As the interval of the log is 7781 add 2351
to 7781. The answer is 1.0132.

Find the anti-log of 1.10132 and the nearest number
in the table is 1.0122. Run your pencil up the column

and the number of degrees is 2. The number opposite minutes is 20.

As the noon position of the Moon on the 30th is 24° 7', subtract 2° 20' from this and the result is 21° 47', which is the Moon's position at the time of birth.

Calculating the positions of the remaining planets is easier because the distances they travel are much smaller. All you have to do is to divide the daily motion by one sixth, or the interval between noon and the time of birth.

Mercury
Daily motion is 0° 46'
minus 0° 24' =   0° 22'
Divide 22 by 6 = 3.6 or roughly   0° 04'
Position on 30th is 0° 46'
minus 0° 4' =   0° 42'   ♏

Venus
Daily motion is
4° 40' minus 3° 27' =   1° 13'
Divide 1° 13' by 6 = 12.08
or roughly   0° 12'
Position on 30th is 4° 40'
minus 0° 12' =   4° 28'   ♏

Mars
Daily motion is 5° 27'
minus 4° 51' =   0° 37'
Divide 0° 37' by 6 =   0° 06'
Position on 30th is 5° 28'
minus 0° 6' =   5° 22'   ♍

Neptune
As the daily motion is only 0° 1'
write down   24° 35'   ♏

Uranus
As the daily motion is only 0° 3'
write down   0° 07'   ♎

Saturn
As the daily motion is only 0° 4'
write down   23° 15'   ♈ **R**

Jupiter
As the daily motion is only 0°
13' write down   21° 00'   ♍

Pluto
Pluto's movement is so slow that it is given only once
in 10 days. The positions will be found on page 39.
Between 27 September and 30 October Pluto travelled
0° 21'. If in 10 days Pluto travelled 0° 21' then in 3 days
it travelled 21 × 33 divided by 10 = 6.3 or roughly 0°
6'. Therefore, its position on the 30th is 21 minus 6 or
23° 13' ♍.

Positions of Planets in the Chart
It will be seen that each planet comes under one of the
signs and its precise position will be determined by the
number of degrees and/or minutes it travels in 24 hours.
The house into which it falls will be determined by the
degrees of the sign it occupies. Thus it will be seen that
♂ falls into the tenth house and as the position of ♂ is
5° 22' it will be nearer the cusp of the house.

Saturn is in ♈ but you will see that in the tables on
page 19, on the 2nd, when it is 24° 7', there is the letter
R in the column, which means Retrograde. Mark that
into your chart. You will also see that the column starts
with 25° 0' and the number of degrees grows smaller
till at the foot of the column we have 23° 15'. The planet
does not really travel backwards but merely appears to

do so because of its relative movement with the earth. Every planet can become retrograde; the Sun and Moon cannot. So write Saturn into your chart as 23° 15′ ♈ ℞. As 23° 15′ is near 27½° place it near the cusp.

Similarly ♃ and ♇ which are 21° 00′ and 23° 14′ respectively, will be placed in the eleventh house; so with ♅ and ☉; but at the other end of the house ♆, ♀ and ☿ are all in the first house, and as ♆ is 24° 35′ it will be placed nearer the cusp.

Aspects
The houses remain fixed. The signs move clockwise through them, and the planets counter-clockwise through the signs.

When the planets are in position it will be possible to see how they are aspected. The Moon, for instance, is 90° from ♄ so it is square with it, and 120° (trine) with ♃. It is also trine with ♇ and ♃.

The Declinations of the planets will be found on pages 18 and 19 in the columns marked Dec under the names of the planets. Uranus is called Herschel, the name of the astronomer who discovered the planet.

The Declinations of the Sun and Moon will be found in the tables in the bottom half of page 18 under ☉ Dec and ☽ Dec. Fill these into the Table of Aspects, as shown.

The Nodes
The positions of the Nodes are given on page 19 under the column Nodes with the sign of the ☽ above it. The Node here refers to the North Node ☊, so write that into the table and place the South Node ☋ exactly opposite.

Parallels
A planet with a declination within 2 of another planet is said to be 'in parallel'. If the declination of each is N (north) or S (south) this is similar in effect to a

conjunction. When one is N and the other S the effect is that of an opposition.

Table of Aspects

By using your judgement you can fill in the table of aspects and this, together with the chart, will enable you to assess the character and potentialities of the native.

Do not imagine that because you can erect a chart you are an astrologer. It is estimated that a million people in American can, but few go any further. That is just the start of a journey into a new and fascinating study which will become increasingly interesting as your grasp increases. There are many books to read which will increase your knowledge and, as with all arts and sciences, the more you learn the more you will want to know.

If you are a parent, astrology will help you in the development and education of your children; if you marry it will help you better to understand your partner; if in business, to sum up your colleagues; and if you run your own business it could enable you to determine who among your prospective employees are best suited to the kind of work you offer and are most likely to prove loyal and efficient. All this, providing you know the date of birth; and better still, the time and place.

Note

Take care to write the symbols for the planets and signs so that they cannot be mistaken. If badly written ♎ can be mistaken for ♒; ♄ for ♃; ♍ for ♏; ☿ for ♀; ♆ for ♅; ♓ for ♉; and ♌ for the North Node ☊.

INDEX